At the Mouth of a Cannon

Conquest and Cupidity on Canada's West Coast: A Personal Account

by Kevin D. Annett

January, 2018

Published under the conditions of the Common Cause Copyright Agreement.

This book and its contents may be reproduced, duplicated, quoted and otherwise cited, in whole or in part, for non-commercial purposes, provided the author is acknowledged.

When you enter into the land of the people you are to possess and you have defeated them, you must destroy them totally. Make no treaty with them and show them no mercy. Tear down their altars and destroy their sacred images. Let none of them live. For you are a people chosen by the Lord over all others on the face of the earth.
    - The Bible, Deuteronomy Chapter 7

Our ancestors obtained the kingdom thus, the very lands we all along enjoyed, they ravished from the people they destroyed; from them our large possessions we enjoy, and time makes the wrong no less. Thus all our fathers' villainies we crown, approve their crimes, and make them all our own; and these must help us claim a right divine, by blood, by rapes, by robberies proclaimed. Religion's always on the strongest side.
    - Jure Divino, Daniel Defoe , 1706

It is obvious that the local savages surrendered their lands only at the mouth of a cannon, and I suppose this will account for their eventual disappearance. The consequence upon any people when confronted by a superior nation is always the same everywhere, and British Columbia is no exception.
    - Provincial Land Commissioner Gilbert Sproat commenting on the Ahousaht Indian tribe, Port Alberni, 1868

Table of Contents

Dedication

Introduction - The Innocents in the Abattoir

Chapter One - In the Beginning: The Place called Ahousaht

Chapter Two - The Pale Plague: Slash, Steal, Repeat

Chapter Three - It's all about the Real Estate, Mate: Land Grabs and Death Camps

Chapter Four - John Ross versus the Maquinnas

Interlude - All in the Family

Chapter Five - Showdown on the Coast: A Tale of Two Letters and A Takeover

Chapter Six - Opening the Floodgates: The Little Matter of Genocide

Chapter Seven - Aftermath: What is this Thing called Neo-Colonialism?

Denouement - A Post-Canadian Reflection

Footnotes

Documents

Appendix One - A Chronology of the Crime

Appendix Two - An Important Note on Sources

A Brief Anthology of works on the Ahousahts and related matters

About the Author

Note to the reader: All of the crimes and incidents described in these pages are based on my personal experience, documented evidence and witness testimonies compiled over twenty years and archived at www.murderbydecree.com .

As Bertrand Russell observed, the problem with uncovering official secrets is never a lack of proof but the willingness to disbelieve. We have furnished you with the proof; belief or denial, and what you will do with either, is up to you.

Dedication

To the members of my Port Alberni community, native and pale, who exposed the three-headed monster that devoured the Ahousaht people and their land. Their sacrifice and their witness endures.

And to Chief Earl Maquinna George of the Ahousaht Nation, who stayed true to himself and to his ancestors.

Introduction: The Innocents in the Abattoir

Those of you who have read some of my other books know that my life as a west coast clergyman ended abruptly one October morning in 1994 when I discovered a well kept secret. In one sense, it's odd how much of a secret it was, considering how it involved entire nations and vast old growth forests. But this is Canada, after all.

Oscar Wilde observed that whoever looks beneath the surface of things does so at his own risk. That's true enough, but thin comfort after the fact – especially since where the veneer ends and the hidden begins is rarely clear at first to the surface dwellers. To my novice eyes, Port Alberni seemed like just another struggling west coast lumber mill town, and my congregation the usual crowd of pale, preoccupied church goers. The scenery of this drama was ordered and secure; Indians and felonious history still waited in the wings.

Nevertheless, the scent of something else wafted into our snug sanctuary early in my tenure at St. Andrew's United Church. It came in an idle remark about the local Indians from the aged chairman of my church board, one Sunday morning during coffee hour: *"They keep to themselves and we keep to ourselves, Kevin. Everybody likes it that way."*

As a former town mayor whose family had been among the first white settlers to the Alberni valley, old Fred Bishop seemed to know what he was talking about when it came to the local brown folks. The Indians rarely if ever ventured over Port Alberni's unspoken color-bar, staying ensconced in the town's slum district or on the nearby but obscure reservations. But Fred's answer to my query about why there were no Indians in our church seemed like no answer at all.

Perhaps it was that sense of mystery surrounding Fred's words that prompted me to step outside my own snug bubble that same week. My movement was assisted by a providential phone call I received from one of those Others: a man named Danny Gus, a retired native fisherman who wanted me to perform his wedding. He belonged to the ancient tribe called the Ahousahts who had once numbered in the tens of thousands. Danny invited me to his home.

The hidden hand appeared briefly that day, outstretched and gnarled.

....

The same uninformed condition that brings anyone into a church was responsible for my arrival in the land of the Ahousahts. Something in my unguarded approach to other people seemed to attract struggling souls to me. Foremost in that sense were Indians.

I didn't know at the time how the apparently fawning approach towards whites displayed by many of Port Alberni's aboriginals was in fact part of the elaborate camouflage they'd learned to adopt to protect what was left of themselves. Visibly strong, independent or intelligent Indians didn't last long a century ago, nor do they today. If they have survived, it has been by playing the victim.

In turn, the pretense is reciprocated by my people. White Canadians can only relate to everyday Indians as a stereotype, either as needy people in a state of dependency or domesticated media icons. So it took some time before I saw past the appearances and the co-dependent lie that everyone has such a vested interest in sustaining.

On the few occasions when they did meet, the pale and dark populaces in our town relied on each other to keep the fragile fiction intact. Certain topics were always avoided. White people gave every Indian the same wary grimace that passed for a smile, as if that would prevent bad feelings or forbidden topics, or erase the carnage. The natives in turn knew how to pump White Guilt to the maximum to get whatever they thought they needed at any given moment. Nobody was honest, for that might disclose the dragon in the living room.

Despite this careful etiquette, whiffs of something else began to find their way to me, no doubt because of my curiousity that was sparked by Fred Bishop's remark. Prompted thus, I began to explore the local terrain with the street smarts of a six year old, crossing the color bars and no-go boundaries that run like invisible ley lines throughout the Alberni Valley. And so through what seemed at the time like a random encounter did I begin to learn something of the real deal.

"They killed my best friend in their residential school".

Danny Gus stared at me with solemn brown eyes that seemed surprised by his own words, spoken to me, of all people. I set aside the noxious plate of chummis – salmon eggs in oil – that I had pretended to enjoy.

"He's buried in the hill behind the school. The whites all know it and that's why they don't want us in their churches"

The sagging Ahousaht man turned to his newly-wed wife Clothilda, who had just brought in more tea. They held themselves away from me but with a subtle look of hope.
Danny's words weighed on me like the foreign mush in my stomach. Later, alone in my basement study, I wondered what it all meant. My tutoring in the real and not imagined nature of my people and our history would be a long and tortured re-learning. Eventually it would cost me my old life and launch a new one. But my real education began, as in all things, with the land itself.

The Ahousaht Homeland: Maaqtusiis **Village, Clayoquot Sound**
(including Lot 363, right foreground)

They seemed strange to us, people without a land of their own.

We asked them "Why are you lost?".

- Maquinna, Siem of the Ahousahts, on first contact

with Europeans, 1778

It is a land of terrifying storms and of hidden dangers, fit only for the beast and the savage. Only the harshest measures will allow us to civilize these heathens and save those we can.

    - Roman Catholic missionary Auguste-Joseph Brabant, Ahousaht, 1874

The Ahousahts are among the most aggressive and impudent savages on the coast.

    - Anglican missionary and Indian Agent Harry Guillod, 1903

Chapter One: In the Beginning - The Place called Ahousaht

The storm-swept land fronts on the Pacific Ocean and gives the People their name Ahousaht, which means "facing the sea". That much we know. But the truth is that nobody can remember what it was really like before the Conquest: not even the Ahousahts themselves.

There are barely a couple of thousand of them remaining now, where once there were possibly thirty times that number. Their language, which comes from the land, is held in remnant pieces by the survivors of the survivors, and is fractured into local dialects that may vary only a few kilometers apart.

The Ahousahts' own oral accounts of their history are very fragmentary and inseparable from myth, and are disputed even in their own ranks. Their tribe is divided into seven local bands dispersed on twenty five tiny ghettos called reservations. Those who claim to know who these People originally were are speaking of an imagined history from an equally imagined authority.

The People believe they have lived in what is called the Clayoquot Sound since the beginning of time, from the moment when (according to one of their many creation stories) an original male and female ancestor joined hands through their separate abodes in ocean surf bubbles, sprang onto a beach near Friendly Cove and together made the first Ahousaht people. Pale archaeologists suggest a five thousand year occupation. Regardless of the true time line, the People hunted whales and fished the seas and rivers for millenia. Like all coastal tribes they once relied on the once-gargantuan cedar trees for nearly everything, from their clothes to their homes, boats, tools and medicines. (1)

As among every obliterated people, the Ahousahts only came into historical focus after their Conquerers arrived in the year 1778, when British seaman James Cook dropped in to say hello. That's the official line, at least. The Ahousahts speak of "the whites before the whites": perhaps Sir Walter Raleigh, if you believe some, or various lost or wandering Asian fishermen, or maybe even Vikings, scooting down from a northern ice-free passage during a warmer, less glaciated age. It's all conjecture. What is certain is the fitting name the

Ahousahts gave to the early Pale tourists who parked on their shores: *Mu-Multh-Nee*, which translates as The Ones without a Home, or The Ghost People.

Names are funny things, and usually tell us more about the Namer than the thing they're labelling. Legend has it that the British appelation for these People they encountered - "Nootka" - was adopted after Jim Cook and his boys heard the local people mumbling that word. Figuring with standard European myopia that that's what the Indians called themselves, Cook didn't realize the term actually meant "You are lost" or "What are you doing here?".

Ghost People, indeed.

The British soon jostled and bayoneted-out the Russians and the Spaniards – who briefly laid a claim on the area – and began to spread their spectral presence about the west coast. By the 1840's Rule Brittania had worked out a border with the Americans that gave all of "Vancouver Island" to England. The first British colony was then promptly established in 1849 in what became Victoria: not coincidentally, the same year that the whites discovered gold on the west coast. And then the *Mu-Multh-Nee* invasion really began, and the Ahousahts started to die en masse.

The three waves of smallpox that wiped out most of the remaining Ahousahts between 1862 and 1895 were neither accidental nor Acts of God. On the contrary, they were the actions of the Hudson's Bay Company, its subsidiary the Puget Sound Agricultural Company (PSAC), and their political backers and fellow PSAC shareholders in the colonial government.

Like elsewhere in what became British Columbia, germ warfare was deliberately introduced among local Indian tribes by vaccine-bearing missionaries – men like "Reverend" John Sheepshanks of the Anglican Church of Canada. Sheepshanks was a clerical hitman and an insider with the government. He was also a PSAC investor and colonial land agent who in the summer of 1864 personally killed off about 90% of the interior Chilcotin people after innoculating them with smallpox. His fellow PSAC shareholders then occupied the lands emptied by the priest. (2)

Please note, if you will, this trinity of church, state and business that manifests in so many frontier agents of the Canadian genocide; for it is a centre piece of this story and will appear time and again, especially among the more isolated and independent Ahousaht people.

Church missionaries were normally granted by the British "Crown" not only huge swaths of other peoples' land but the power of a magistrate, a policeman and a land broker, and they often operated their own lucrative logging, fur or fishing companies on the side. This fact placed vast tracts of never-ceded indigenous lands and their resources in the filthy paws of the Catholic, Anglican and (later) United Church of Canada. Together, these churches led the final extermination of the native nations in their misnamed "Indian residential schools". Thus does the plot thicken, and sicken.

In the way of a foreshadowing, witness if you will the arrival in the Ahousaht heartland of a white man in a boat one spring morning in 1891: a Presbyterian missionary named Melvin Swartout. His uninvited descent on the Ahousahts has caused more of an upset among his fellow whites than the natives;

especially to a similarly-intrusive Roman Catholic priest named Auguste-Joseph Brabant, who twenty years earlier had laid claim to all of the Ahousahts and their neighbouring tribes as part of his "flock". In a letter to the government demanding that the Protestant intruder be barred from the Ahousaht territory, Brabant accuses Swartout and his church of "poaching".

The animal reference is fitting, for by then the Ahousahts, like the sea otters, are close to extinction.

Even the most obtuse government-sponsored account of the west coast genocide acknowledges the extremely rapid pace by which smallpox wiped out entire west coast Indian cultures.

According to the collaborationist, state-allied "Indigenous Corporate Training Incorporated", half the coastal native population was wiped out in one year: "It's estimated that, prior to the 1862 smallpox epidemic, there were about 30,000 First Nations living on the coastline of BC, post-epidemic that number drops to 15,000." (3). This typically low Euro-

Canadian estimate of aboriginal numbers obscures the fact that the seeds of the depopulation of many hundreds of thousands of Indians had been planted on the west coast soon after first contact in 1778. Many of the coastal Indians had already died by the mid 19th century. Even the state-managed and censored Wikipedia admits that "From earliest contact with European explorers up until 1830, more than 90% of the west coast Nuu-chah-nulth confederacy died as a result of infectious disease epidemics." (4)

Like many other tribes, the Ahousahts began to fight back after most of their people had been killed off by the plague. In the same year of 1864, when the smallpox deaths had peaked across the province, both the Ahousahts and the Chilcotin people of central B.C. did battle with white settlers and travelling agents of death like John Sheepshanks. In response, nine coastal Ahousaht villages were bombarded and partly destroyed by Royal Navy gunships. And hot on the heels of this germ and cannoneering warfare came the missionary invasion.

The Catholics arrived first, naturally. One of them, a Jesuit missionary named Paul Durieu, cooked up the original blueprint for corraling and eliminating all the independent aboriginals on the west coast. The Durieu Plan was a rehashing of a very old Roman strategy, which was to wipe out the traditional leaders of any targeted group and elevate new converts among the conquered to a false authority in the indigenous villages. A "Watchman" system of spying on and eliminating any lingering traditionalists was then established. Its main purpose was to complete the eradication of the conquered by imprisoning and brainwashing the next generation of their own people to be servants of the conquerors, in special internment camps deceptively named Indian schools.

This technique worked flawlessly at destroying the identity of the Indians and killing off their real leaders. Soon the Canadian government and the Protestant churches followed suit, and the "Indian residential school" system was born.
Auguste Brabant, who so despised the rival Presbyterians who also laid claim to the Ahousahts, set up Catholic Indian villages all over the west coast. The priest conducted a one

man reign of terror for decades, imprisoning any Indian who resisted his plan to make them little Roman clones. Unfortunately for Mr. Brabant and his gang, the Ahousahts didn't take to "conversion" or to Durieu's scheme.

Of all the British Columbia tribes, the Ahousahts remained themselves the longest. As late in the invasion calendar as 1904, only two of the 273 surviving Ahousahts in the main Maaqtusiis reserve were Christians. Even when two Indian residential schools had been opened among them, a majority of the Ahousahts remained non-Christian. This local native resistance set off alarm bells in church, business and government circles, all of whom wanted the remaining Indians off their land and safely domesticated. *(See Figure 1 and Footnote 5)*

We'll explore how this all played out in later chapters. For now, the Ahousaht example is important to note, since it determined the actions of the church-state-corporate octopus that increasingly wound itself around British Columbia as the 20th century bloodily unfolded.

....

The man's English name was Nelson Keitlah, quite possibly because his real name was either unknown to himself or unpronounceable. Like any modern Ahousaht politician he had learned to appear to straddle two separate worlds. Nelson was a traditional *siem* or elder of his people, and the first Indian to take up my offer to join our congregation of St. Andrew's United Church. Indian-style, he brought most of his family with him.

Despite receiving various discourtesies from some of the pale parishioners – including queries as to whether he was on welfare or where exactly in the local slums he lived – Nelson kept returning to our church services and even took a liking to me. One Sunday after our worship service he invited me to his elegant home for tea; thankfully, without the chummis included.

I didn't know at the time what a big wheel Nelson was in the provincial aboriginal leadership; at least, among those "leaders" who had been rubber stamped for approval by the government's treaty negotiators. Regardless, the man carried himself with a natural dignity normally absent among most of the so-called tribal leaders. And so he waited calmly as we sipped our tea, taking my measure in silence.

"I can see you are genuinely interested in who we are" Nelson said quietly. "I can see you don't want to take something from us."

Much was said in his not saying it. He sat back and shut his eyes before speaking.

His people did not have a name for the woman when she appeared to them, many lifetimes before the whites. Only when she gave them her teachings did she reveal herself.

"She warned us that pale skinned people would come in her name to our land, people who held only some of her way but not the most important part, about respect and equality, of being on the same level with all other people" Nelson explained. "She told us to welcome the strangers and to show them the real spirit of her teachings."

"Secret teachings?" I asked, remembering a sermon on the

Gnostic Gospels I'd just given to my skeptical congregation.

"They're just a secret to the whites" Nelson remarked gently. I smiled at his remark, knowing how likely it was that Christ would have manifested as a woman to the matrilineal Ahousahts.

Nelson's disclosure soon gave me a thump where it mattered. For I realized with a shock how the entire basis for my culture's claim to aboriginal land was in fact completely erroneous. We had not brought the Gospels to the Indians: quite the opposite, in fact.

"Then I guess us whites had better just pack up and leave" I said jokingly to Nelson. But he didn't smile. Instead, he deepened my education. Later that month, Nelson first mentioned to me the name of Earl Maquinna George. Nelson Keitlah may have been their political head-man, but Earl was the heartbeat of the Ahousahts.

As a direct descendant of Chief Maquinna, a quasi-legendary warrior-leader of the Ahousahts, Earl's official title was the hereditary Keeper of the Land, the *Tyee Ha'wiih*. As such his sacred duty was to prevent the destruction of the lands given to the Ahousahts by their Creator. But being so charged placed Earl George in direct collision with not only rapacious logging companies and their United Church and government business partners, but with Earl's own Ahousaht Tribal Council, whose fat cat "chiefs" wanted a proverbial piece of the action. That was the situation when Nelson mentioned Earl's name to me early in 1993. And then I began to learn some of the real history of the Ahousahts, at the eventual cost of everything I knew and loved.

Once again, I'm getting ahead of the story. Suffice it to say that the Ahousahts have been at the centre of the storm that is the west coast Canadian Genocide. And yet something in the mist-shrouded coves and islands seems to have held on to what has always been there.

....

If he still walked the earth, Harry Guillod would be known among other things as an efficient multi-tasker. He was a church man, a businessman and a government Indian agent all rolled into one. He was also an Adolf Eichmann-like facilitator of mass murder.

Harry Guillod began his adult years in the mid 19th century as a Church of England missionary to the west coast Indian tribes. In that position he peformed the same fatal role in relation to the Ahousahts that his Anglican clerical colleague John Sheepshanks did among the Chilcotin Indians – and during the same years of the middle 1860's - when Sheepshanks spread smallpox among them through lethal injections.

Harry Guillod was dispatched among the most independent and disease-free of the coastal tribes, the Huu-ay-aht band of the Ahousahts. Shortly after his arrival among the Huu-ay-ahts in the fall of 1868, Guillod reported to his Anglican bosses that the "rapidly spreading" disease had already killed forty Huu-ay-ahts and the Indians preferred to starve during the winter than live with the disease. Later, Guillod said that 90% of the natives in the Clayoquot, Barkley and Nootka Sounds were dead from smallpox. (6)

As with John Sheepshanks, Harry Guillod was soon rewarded

for his efforts by his fellow Anglicans who ran the provincial government. Appointed as a district Indian Agent despite his paucity of qualifications, Guillod used the position to "pre-empt" aboriginal land from their original owners who were all soon to conveniently die from smallpox. Harry Guillod became a very wealthy man, opening and running Port Alberni's first sawmill and overseeing the launching of the first Indian residential schools in the area.

Being a loyal church-state-company man with a vested interest in hiding his own bloody deeds, Harry Guillod didn't like the resilient Ahousaht Indians very much, since they were surviving witnesses to the crime after many of the other tribes had succumbed to it. And so Guillod expanded the missionary assault on the Ahousahts in the early 1890's by encouraging the aforementioned Presbyterian cleric Melvin Swartout to go among them and plant a mission and school there and in Port Alberni – much to the chagrin of the Catholic priest Auguste Brabant. Guillod in fact made the Ahousahts the main target of church and state assaults as the residential school era began in the last decade of the 19th century. By 1950, there were only a couple of hundred

Ahousahts left alive.

Perhaps Nelson Keitlah's story of Christ's sojourn among his people before the whites arrived was true. Whatever it is that sustained their remnant continues to abide in the margins, even as the genocide that worked so well has made the present-day Ahousaht "chiefs" land profiteers and criminals in their own right.

Harry Guillod's legacy is still remembered by the remnant. In the hilltop cemetery that overlooks the former United Church Indian residential school west of Port Alberni, Guillod's headstone rests in overgrown obscurity. A few years ago, someone smashed it to pieces.

To invade, search out, capture, vanquish and subdue all Saracens and Pagans whatsoever, and other enemies of Christ wheresoever placed, and to reduce their persons to perpetual slavery.

> \- Papal Bull <u>Romanus Pontifex</u> (1455) that authorized the genocide of the non-Catholic world *(Note: This Bull has never been revoked)*

Colonization is civilization. If we, the superior race, take the land of other races, we must utterly destroy the previous inhabitants.

> \- Sir Edward Bulwer-Lytton, co-founder of British Columbia and Member of the Legislative Assembly, 1868

I just got a blanket well-infected with smallpox and put it between my saddle blanket and a sweat pad. I went into all their villages with it and I succeeded. All of the savages died of smallpox.

> \- John McLain, Hudson's Bay Company trader and land speculator, on his trips among the Chilcotin indians, <u>Only in Nazko</u> (1908)

I believe the conditions are being deliberately created in our Indian schools to spread infectious diseases. The death rate often exceeds fifty percent. This is a national crime.
    - Dr. Peter Bryce to Indian Affairs Deputy Superintendent Duncan Campbell Scott, April 12, 1907

Genocide does not necessarily mean the immediate or the total physical destruction of an entire nation. It is rather a coordinated plan of different actions aiming at the eventual annihilation of the group by destroying the essential foundations of their life.
    - Raphael Lemkin, <u>Axis Rule in Occupied Europe</u> (1944)

It's always been about the land. They had to kill us or make us forget who we are so they could have the land. It didn't matter how many of us had to die. It didn't bother the whites one bit when they were doing that to us and it still doesn't.
    - Nuu-Chah-Nulth elder and Alberni residential school survivor Harriett Nahanee, December 23, 1995

When plunder becomes a way of life for a group of men in a society, over the course of time they create for themselves a legal system **that authorizes it** and a moral code **that glorifies it.**

Frederic Bastiat

Chapter Two: The Pale Plague – Slash, Steal, Repeat

It all begins with a simple issue: Can anyone own the earth and its people? If not, it is because nature and human beings are naturally free and have the right to remain themselves. But if by some strange device both creation and humanity can be parceled out to the highest bidder like merchandise, it follows that the possessors have the right to do whatever they want to what they "own": including destroy it.

The ancient Hebrews, Greeks and Romans were in agreement on this issue. Their societies answered a big "yes" to whether the earth and other human beings could be possessed; and an equally definite "no" to whether people have the right to remain themselves. They all believed that the earth had been given to some of mankind to be possessed so that it could be cultivated and "improved", and in the process help perfect those human beings who were stronger, more worthy or divinely chosen over others.

Since so-called western civilization arose from these cultures, their notions of the nature and rights of property, the earth and humanity were directly responsible for that little matter of genocide that sprouted from their ranks.

The oldest, that is Hebrew, attitude on all of this arose from a single foundational narrative, the creation story in the Book of Genesis. The original translation of Genesis describes a huge war in heaven that destroyed and then divided creation into two warring parts, that of light and of darkness. Into this cosmic battlefield a mysterious group called the Eloyhim deposited one of their inventions, a slave race called mankind. The latter were to care for the world in the name of their masters. Instead, the people woke up to their servitude and revolted.

Like masters tend to do, the Eloyhim overlords took offense at this defiance and banished humanity into a harsh and unforgiving world. People were then pitted against each other: man against woman, tribe against tribe, cult against cult. In the process, mankind subjugated and despoiled the world in the name of a new ruler (or was it just the old one under a new title?) named Jehovah.

By the tenth century BC, what arose from this founding story and philosophy was a militarized, slave-owning monarchy, "the Land of Israel". It was a society where the land was a perpetual battlefield to be conquered by the strongest, along with any people not in the Hebrews-only, Jehovah-worshipping club.

Some centuries later and not far to the west, classical Greek culture arose on a very similar philosophical basis to the Hebrews, in part because of their trade and contact with Israel and Judea. The big difference with the Greeks is that they were polytheistic, but the nature of their gods was every bit as perverse as the Eloyhim/Jehovah mono-divinity: warlike, cruel, vengeful and oppressive when it came to creation and mankind. People were mere puppets in divine hands, and as with the Hebrews, this alleged "divinely ordained" master-slave relationship was projected onto all of Greek society.

The fourth century BC Greek philosopher Aristotle, who not coincidentally was the tutor of the fellow who led the conquest of most of the known world while still in his twenties – Alexander the Great – put it all this way: There is a natural division and hierarchy in creation that subordinates some to others because of their different natures. The slave is a slave because he is born that way, as one who is naturally inferior to the slave master, and therefore will always be in a subordinate position. The same is true of people who are conquered in war: they are naturally inferior and so faced defeat in battle.

Because of this so-called nature of things, Aristotle – and his own teacher Plato, whose philosophy the Church of Rome loved so much - concluded that those who are superior have a natural right to possess everything and everyone, whether that be the land itself or the people, plants and animals in it, and to use them however they choose.

In short, there are no inherent rights or liberties. The status of everyone and everything is determined and fixed by their nature, which makes most people objects in the hands of those who are innately superior. The latter, of course, just so happened to be the wealthy and the strong. (7)

The Romans may have militarily conquered the Greeks in the second century BC but the culture of the latter osmosified into their new masters. Rome developed and organized Aristotle's ideas into legal codes that governed not just the law but politics and every aspect of life in first the Roman Republic, and then the Empire.

Roman law developed the first precise notion of property as "chattel" and applied it to people as well as to things. A man or woman's nature and status in society was defined by the law and not by one's inherent, indwelling condition.

Because of this, that social status could be altered in order to reduce or diminish someone's standing under the law. People in effect were moveable goods, the property of others, especially if they were foreigners, prisoners of war or born into slavery.

The Roman legal term for this reduction of legal condition was *capitis diminutio* ("decrease of head"), and had three degrees: *capitis diminutio minima, media and maxima.*

The smallest reduction of status, *capitis diminutio minima*, indicated a loss of family membership, as when a child grew up and moved out from under paternal authority, but his liberties and citizenship remained. The next level of diminishing, *media,* occured when citizenship was lost along with family identity, but personal liberty remained. The most degraded state, *capitis diminutio maxima,* meant the stripping of all three – family, citizenship and personal liberty – and applied to slaves and those conquered in war. This state meant complete bondage: legally, such a person did not exist. (8)

This third condition is of great relevance to our story, for it was a status that was automatically applied by the Roman state – and by its descendent, the Church of Rome – to all people outside their Empire. As early as the fourth century, that Church declared that those who were not Catholics were in a <u>non-existent condition,</u> as was the land they occupied. **Such people were *Nullus*, or <u>nothing</u>,** under Church-Roman law, and could be legally killed and their nation eradicated. Similarly, their land was considered to be *Terra Nullus*: "the land of no-one", and could be seized and claimed by any

Catholic ruler. If such people converted to Catholicism they came into legal existence and acquired a limited humanity. They could then be enslaved but not arbitrarily killed. (9)

Every European missionary that came to foreign shores, and to the west coast of Canada, was infused with this belief and legal system. But the methods employed against the indigenous people by Catholics and Protestants differed. The former absorbed converts directly into a Catholic mini-theocratic state, set up on native land to supplant and destroy the traditional society. Protestants, conversely, sought to politically incorporate their Indian converts into their own nation-state and make them "good Canadian citizens", according to Martin Luther's "Two Swords" theory of church-state partnership. (10)

Regardless of these different methods, the genocidal result was always the same. Its primary target was not simply the natives but their land. In the words of west coast Anglican missionary and Indian Agent Harry Guillod, written in 1889,

"A man does not lose his land because he is a slave; he

becomes a slave because he has lost his land. To talk of the rights of the Indians is therefore pointless."

This fact was recognized early on in the colonial era, by the Churches of Rome and of England. Vatican lawyers devised a legal justification for stealing non-Catholic lands whereby in return for receiving "Christianity" (that is, Papist authority), the conquered people surrendered their lands and themselves into a voluntary servitude. This same general formula was used by the British Crown when it conquered much of Ireland during the 16th and 17th centuries. But because the subjugated Irish were Catholics, England invented a policy of "surrender and reissue" that allowed local tribal rulers, once they had capitulated to the Crown, to keep their religious beliefs and continue to govern but under a new, Crown authority and jurisdiction. The same arrangement governed Quebec after the British Conquest of 1763.

In other words, the land was claimed, captured and owned by England but "reissued" to and administered for the Crown by local rulers. This ingenious practice allowed England to win mastery over one quarter of the world's population through an apparent liberality that masked the same old policy of conquest and land grab. **The practice co-opted the surviving tribal leaders into the administration of the British Empire and gave them a stake in their own enslavement by granting them a limited authority over their own land that had been "reissued" to them.**

This ingenious model of conquest is the one that has been used by Canada towards "its" aboriginal nations and remains in place under the Indian Act and the tribal council system. The latter administers the land <u>for</u> the Crown, which holds the title to all lands in Canada by right of their being "vested in Her Majesty in perpetuity" – that is, forever. *(see The Indian Act of Canada, RSC 1985).*

This system was formalized in Canada in 1857 by a law known as the Gradual Civilization Act. It stated that aboriginals had no legal standing and would not be recognized until they had "enfranchised" themselves by surrendering their lands and traditional rights. In return, they would be given a piece of land no larger than fifty acres that was owned by the Crown.

But even then they were not considered citizens, and could neither vote nor sue in court.

In short, under the guise of "granting" land to the Indians, such enfranchisement in fact cemented Indians in Canada into a sub-standard legal category of non-citizenship that continues today under the Indian Act of Canada. (11)

Regardless of the methods or feigned "benevolence" of colonial conquest, it was always preceded by an opening phase of outright extermination of on average three quarters or more of the original populations. As mentioned, the Ahousahts and other tribes in what became British Columbia lost well over 90% of their pre-contact numbers because of deliberately introduced smallpox epidemics, once they had lost their economic usefulness as mediators of the fur and whaling trade.

In other words, the first act of the missionaries was not religious conversion but extermination and land seizure.

This fact is evident in the creation of the Clergy Reserve system by the British Crown in Canada. Under it, any Christian missionary who camped in an area and began a mission there was immediately granted title and control over hundreds of acres of land around them, regardless of who lived there. These and adjacent lands could then be legally "pre-empted" by the churches.

This legalization of Christian land theft was accompanied by the granting of extremely broad powers to church missionaries by the British authorities as well as the Vatican. Every Catholic priest had the power of life and death over non-Catholics, including the right to arrest, try and execute anyone they chose, and to create church courts and "tribal police" to arrest "heretics". They could also seize any land and property and act as commercial brokers.

Similarly, the Canadian government made Protestant missionaries a direct arm of the state. Church of England missionaries like the infamous Harry Guillod were also Indian Agents and land speculators, and along with their Presbyterian-Methodist and later United Church colleagues, were often appointed as local tax collectors and Magistrates or Justices of the Peace. The founding charter of the United Church of Canada, formed by Parliament in 1925, grants that church the power of a bank and a real estate company, including the right to make loans, issue promissory notes, buy and sell land and operate under their own self-administered laws. The church can even enforce debt collection and operate its own closed church courts that are not subject to review by any civil court in Canada!(*See a copy of the Act at http://www.axz.ca/act.htm , and Footnote 12)*

That is, in every sense the church missionaries and churches who invaded native lands were a power unto themselves; and for obvious reasons. For as the spear tip of foreign conquerers, the churches' job was to start the genocidal process.

Every religious denomination used the same tried and proven methods to achieve this extermination of non-Christians: by culling down aboriginal numbers, wiping out their identity and securing their lands and resources for the settlers and the corporations that were to follow in their wake. And that pre-eminent church power and criminality did not diminish over time.

....

"You're a good Christian, Ed. You don't have to worry. I only sterilize the pagans"
    – United Church missionary doctor George Darby sr. to coastal Hesquait elder Ed Martin, 1954

Like his church, Oliver Howard wasn't that impressive. Despite having piloted a missionary boat among the coastal Indians for over forty years, he didn't know that much about them. But he was to be my guide around Port Alberni, the week I arrived there with my young family in the summer of 1992.

"What all those bleeding hearts keep forgetting is that we were bringing the Good News to where it wasn't" the flabby old guy remarked, as we drove along River Road, past the Opitchesaht Indian reservation. "These people used to practice cannibalism and human sacrifice until we showed up".

I didn't say anything, for it was all so new to me. And as my predecessor at St. Andrew's United Church, Oliver knew what he was talking about, I assumed.

"That's where the old residential school was" he gestured at a mass of trees on a hill. "It was our real pride and joy"

My only connection to the place he referred to had been as a child, when I helped fund the routine obscenities that went on behind the walls of the Alberni Indian residential school. For every Sunday, I dutifully deposited my dollar in the collection plate at Westworth United Church in Winnipeg. Twenty cents of that obtuse tithing went into the Church's Mission and Service Fund that paid for repeat-offender child killers like Reverend Alfred Caldwell, the residential school Principal, whom Oliver had known all too well. But as accomplices to a crime, neither Oliver nor I seemed troubled by it.

"It looks pretty poor out here" I commented as we drove deeper into the reserve and its sagging, moss-covered shacks. Oliver observed,

"They don't take pride in themselves. It's always just take, take with them."

Oliver Howard was an unlikely character in the drama unfolding around us. For just over two years later, he would unwittingly be the one to prompt me to confront the United Church over its theft of local native land and its murder of children. For in response to Oliver's public denial about that theft, I wrote a letter to the church that triggered my firing but also ignited a national firestorm that would unmask unspeakable crimes and their official concealment. Finding justice, of course, was another matter.

The loyal church men like Oliver Howard who shepherded the genocide of the Ahousahts and others never considered what they did to be either morally wrong or felonious. On the contrary. But for our purposes, the ethical mystery of how slaughter becomes legally and religiously sanctified is central to understanding the institutional arrangement that allows home grown crimes against humanity to occur and persist: especially in Canada.

The truth is that in our country, religion – and specifically, Christian imperialism - was not the handmaiden to politics but rather its directing force. In that sense, genocide in Canada was unique, when compared to similar crimes around the world, by the extent to which it was launched, guided, maintained and then concealed by organized religion: predominantly by the Vatican, the Church of England and the true-blue Canadian United Church. The Canadian Holocaust was undeniably a religious, church-run operation from its inception.

As much as all the evidence points to this simple fact, it's a jarring, unacceptable one for most pale Canadians – atheists included. In the popular mind, "Genocide" is usually associated with war-mongering third world dictators, not one's friendly neighbourhood chapel. It's an attitude that was deliberately crafted by western governments after World War Two, when the United Nations' Convention on the Crime of Genocide was being re-fashioned to fit various political vested interests.

That Convention redefined and narrowed the original

meaning of genocide to mean the physical eradication of groups, rather than (in the original definition) **any act that destroys even some of a people,** like killing their language or trafficking their children out of their families. The final U.N. Convention also made it impossible to prosecute anyone for Genocide unless their government agreed to cooperate. This caveat is no doubt responsible for the fact that since its passing in 1948, the Convention has only been employed twice, and never against aboriginal-killing western powers like the USA, Canada, England and the Vatican.

The inescapable truth is that Genocide is not alien to our culture but is our very own monotheistic religious ideal, arisen from out of Judaeo- Christianity. But being raised within that culture, few of us can see the murk and the blood in which we swim. (13)

The single animating belief behind Judaeo-Christianity and the society it spawned is one of innate superiority over all other faiths and cultures, and a corresponding incompatibility with the rest of humanity. Quite simply, in our tradition other peoples do not have the right to remain themselves. They must conform to our way or be eradicated. And our constant adherence to that genocidal creed is evident in a body count of the untold millions of victims of European Christianity over two millenia.

Historically, what we call genocide has never been a crime nor an aberration in our culture, but rather is a normative tool of European church and state. Indeed, the targeting for destruction of other groups is at the heart of Judaeo-Christianity because it is part of a sacred practice of ritual blood sacrifice that defines who we are as a "people chosen by God". Our holy texts declare time and again that we are cleansed and redeemed by the blood of others.

The roots of this idea are found early in the Bible. The ancient Hebrew word *kiddush* means both "sanctification" and "sacrifice". Similarly, a priest routinely offers "oblations", or sacrifices, to the Almighty, but only of the purest and most innocent creature. For God demanded even the suffering and death of his own perfect Jesus so that all would be saved. One or many virtuous beings must die so that we may be right with God. As the Roman Catholic liturgy instructs,

"Whoever eats of this flesh and drinks of this blood will be purified".

When I first encountered the few brown survivors of our Christian Holocaust, I had no words to explain that our slaughter of them was simply business as usual: a natural expression of our core beliefs. My people may have lusted for their land and its rich bounty, but what brought us among them was a religious devotion that required the extermination of most of their people.

Even though the same belief has been secularized now, that devotion continues to devastate their world and our own.

In Oliver Howard's words, spoken to me as we first toured the Port Alberni Indian reservations in the summer of 1992,

"All their talk of human rights and getting their land back won't mean a thing if they don't mature and come into the twentieth century. Their old way is dead and gone and it's a good thing too."

He's an Anglican Missionary! No, he's an Indian Agent! No, he's a businessman and a land speculator! STOP! You're right, he's all of the above!

Harry Guillod, Creator of many west coast Indian residential schools, c. 1881

I believe the conditions are being deliberately created in our Indian schools to spread infectious disease. The death rate often exceeds fifty per cent. This is a national crime.

    - Dr. Peter Bryce, Chief Medical Officer of Indian Affairs, Ottawa, November 10, 1910

It is remarked that many apparently healthy children on their admission to the different Indian schools are infected with tuberculosis while in the facility and that many of them subsequently die. That the disease is rapidly increasing there is no doubt and if matters are allowed to proceed as they are proceeding today, it will be but a short time before the Indians are wiped out of existence by the disease ...

    - Hayter Reed, Assistant Superintendent for Indian Affairs, Ottawa, April 24, 1897

We appreciate how it is the policy of your Department never to interfere with the work of our missionaries on the Indian Reserves and to expedite our efforts to secure their lands for that work. In that sense, Mr. Scott's recent remarks regarding your policy of achieving a Final Solution to the Indian Problem are reassuring and in accordance with the highest hopes of our

Church.

> - Roman Catholic Archbishop Desmond Orth, Vancouver, to Frank Pedley, Senior Administrator for Indian Affairs, West Coast Agency, January 21, 1904

We have frequently a good deal of trouble with the Indians, growing out of the fact that we have no legal or formal claim to any particular quantity of land ... We ask therefore that the Department should give us a title of occupation protecting us alike from complaints of individual Indians or by the band ... It is most important as well that provision should be made for Boarding Schools and Industrial Institutions where the children can be kept for a series of years away from the influences which surround them on the Reserves. In all cases they must be excluded from the Reserves and to ensure this we must obtain an absolute title to the property.

> - Alexander Sutherland, Secretary of the Methodist Home Mission Society to the Superintendent General of Indian Affairs, Ottawa, March 1, 1888

Chapter Three:
It's all about the Real Estate, Mate – Land Grabs and Death Camps

Even mainstream scholars and government mouthpieces generally agree that the population of indigenous nations in Canada fell to its lowest, near-extinction level by the last quarter of the 19th century. From a pre-contact population of possibly two million people, barely 20,000 of them were alive by that period, according to an 1871 census. *(See Figure 2 and Footnote 14)* The first state authorized Indian residential schools were opened in the same period. There is no coincidence involved. The "schools" were planned as the final knock-out blow against the remnant Indians, especially on the west coast, where remnant "pagans" endured.

By 1891, nearly all of the surviving Indians in British Columbia had been stripped of their traditional lands and forcibly corralled into impoverished concentration camps called reservations. The same year, the federal government began to authorize and subsidize the different church-run Indian schools that dotted the province. Thereafter, "Indian education" became a code word for a joint church-state plan for the final phase of an intergenerational genocide.

The planned, systematic nature of this slaughter has been deliberately obscured by Canada and its churches and has had to be reconstructed from the pieces of a suppressed archival record. (15) But the first indicator of the real purpose of the Indian schools is where they were constructed: in close proximity to rich natural resources in the heartland of the traditional native nations. Of the seventeen residential schools established across B.C. by the Roman Catholic, Anglican and United Church, all but one was located adjacent to the main fishing and hunting grounds of the local Indians or near to major timber and mineral deposits that would one day be seized and exploited by church-allied corporations. (16)

In other words, the rise of the Indian residential school system on Canada's west coast was as much a part of the massive land grab that spanned the years 1849 and 1920 as were the three major smallpox epidemics during the same period. Germ warfare, land theft and residential schools were all part of the same genocidal process that targeted Indians, and cannot be considered in isolation.

"Our purpose given to us by Creator was to guard the forests, the rivers and the animals. To steal it all the whites had to wipe us out or make us forget who we are. That's why they brainwashed us in the residential schools. And it worked.""

The old man who spoke thus was Earl Maquinna George. He was what remained of a traditional Ahousaht elder when I first met him in the spring of 1993.

Earl George is a central character in our tale, as you'll discover. I was nudged in his direction by the aforementioned tribal council chief Nelson Keitlah after the latter started attending my church services; and by a like-minded fellow United Church clergyman, Bruce Gunn, whose pastoral post was among the Ahousahts in their traditional homeland, at the village of Maaqtusiis on the coastal Flores Island.

Bruce had heard about me through the mocassin telegraph, and he must have perked up at the news that a local white clergyman was actually inviting Indians into his church. Soon after Christmas in 1992 after my family and I arrived in Port Alberni, Bruce had invited me out to Maaqtusiis, and into a new world.

Like the hidden history I was about to learn, the sea passage to Flores Island that day was harsh and hazardous. Our boat nearly capsized in the swells sweeping in off the Pacific. But either luck or some invisible hand brought me safely to the village. Bruce Gunn was waiting on the dock, along with a throng of Indians.

"Don't get the wrong idea" Bruce commented with a wry smile as I gazed at the crowd. "They're not here for you. There's a funeral today."

As it turned out, the entire village was on hand to accompany the coffin of the deceased to the local cemetery, children and dogs included. Bruce and I followed at a respectful distance, and nobody seemed to mind.

As we all approached the iron-gated graveyard through the

usual reservation tangle of abandoned cars and foliage run amok, Bruce motioned in the other direction. Soon we were sitting at the back of his church, sipping tea and warming ourselves around a portable heater.

"Earl's on his way over" Bruce remarked.

"Isn't he at the funeral?" I asked, knowing how long an aboriginal burial normally took. Bruce shook his head and grimaced.

"It's a long story. Let's just say there's some bad blood here" Bruce paused and gave me a telling frown. "Earl's a traditionalist. That means he not a popular guy with the band council chiefs."

A wet squall had suddenly descended from out of the west as the wind battered the frail wooden structure, sending blasts of cold air through the floorboards. I was wondering whether I'd get back to Tofino that day when a small, chubby Indian entered the church. He appeared to be in his seventies. He wore a crew cut and a scowl.

After Bruce introduced us, Earl said to me gruffly,
"We don't get many United Church ministers up here. They never stay long. Just long enough to steal something."

I gave him an embarrassed smile as his words hung pregnant in the ether. But then Earl seemed to soften and we all sat down for tea.

The truth seeped out of him slowly as his dark brown eyes probed me . Knowing how asking questions was considered rude by the Ahousahts, I held my tongue and let him say what he would.

I realized quickly that I had landed in the middle of a civil war.

As suited his hereditary role as Keeper of the Land, Earl had just sent a letter to the provincial government that claimed back all of the traditional Ahousaht land that had been stolen by missionaries, including its most lucrative real estate: the old growth red cedar-filled Lot 363, just south of the village. Contrarily, a faction of the Ahousaht band council chiefs were in the process of cooking up an inside deal with the same government to set up their own logging company and grab a piece of the action and the profits.

Meanwhile, the "legal owner" of the Ahousaht land, the big logging company MacMillan-Bloedel, and its financial benefactor and the original land grabber, our very own United Church of Canada, had their own plans. Unbeknownst to anyone but themselves, Mac-Blo and the United Church planned to sell off Lot 363 to the real string puller in this sordid drama, Weyerhauser Ltd. : the world's biggest timber baron. Weyerhauser, in fact, was about to secretly buy up all of MacMillan-Bloedel, and Lot 363 was central to the deal. (17)

To make things even more interesting, just before adopting his oppositional role regarding the United Church's corporate manuevers, Earl George had applied to the same Church for training and ordination as its first west coast aboriginal clergyman. Our local Comox-Nanaimo Presbytery had warmly recommended him and was paying his seminary tuition, and the church public relations aficiandos milked the occasion in their usual whorish manner to "prove" how Indian-friendly the church was.

That is, until Earl wrote his letter.

The details and outcome of this tragic-comedy are spelled out in Chapter Five. Suffice it to say that as Earl and Bruce discussed these machinations on that first day we were together, I felt a sharp petard of indignation rising within me. I was also very confused. Was my church actually a profiteer in stolen native land, when its own politically-correct policy required it to return any such larcenous fruit of conquest to the original owners – in this case, the Ahousahts? And who exactly were the Ahousahts: those traditionalists like Earl George, or the band council clique of imported families known as the Atleos and the Franks, who hoped to make big bucks off the fallen ancient trees on Ahousaht land?

The experience began to force open a locked door for me and set me down a path that would one day threaten to shatter the entire old boy's arrangement between the usual gang of big business, church and state. Meanwhile, I received a rapid education about what my people had done to the

Ahousahts in the name of God and Mammon.

....

The Nazis never called them death camps, but rather special "relocation" or "transportation" centers. Nor has Canadian culture ever referred to its own version of Auschwitz and Buchenwald as anything besides "Indian residential schools". The bare statistics show that over half of the children died in the latter facilities, continually, for nearly a century. The death rate in Auschwitz was much lower, perhaps 15% to 25%. (18)

In the same way that the Nazi genocide started small and mushroomed by what it fed on, so too did the Canadian Holocaust. The earliest Indian schools were normally day operations run by individual missionaries, besides exceptions like the Church of England's Mohawk Residential School in Brantford, Ontario, set up with Crown backing in 1832.

In practice, the missionary day schools failed to capture many children because the Indians were nomadic and seasonal in their movements. In response, all of the churches demanded two things from the state: the funding of permanent "boarding schools" that would warehouse hundreds of children at a time, and a federal law compelling the mandatory attendance of native children in these "schools", on pain of imprisonment or worse. At that point, around 1890, the residential schools genocide began in earnest.

An accurate label for these camps is De-population and Experimental Centers. Their aim was to kill a majority of the incarcerated Indian children and program the surviving minority to be slaves of the colonizers. They succeeded in this aim. The evidence of their intent was present the first year that these state-authorized and church-run camps opened, in an immediately huge death rate. For example, at Catholic Indian schools in Saskatchewan in 1896, two thirds of the entry class had died by the end of that first year of operation. *(See Figures 3 and 4)*

This pattern of an instantly high mortality in Indian schools was constant across western Canada, where most of the facilities were located, and in every religious denomination.

Nor did the huge death rate subside over the subsequent decades, despite constant complaints from doctors and aboriginal families. In response, in the years immediately following the opening of the schools, the government deliberately suppressed and falsified evidence of the high death rate. *(See Figures 5 and 6 and Footnote 19)*

The already-enormous mortality rate continued to rise after all regular medical inspection was actually abolished in these facilites in 1919, and as, over the next decade, the churches were made the sole legal guardians of residential school students, the sexual sterilization of their inmates became legal, and Indians were denied the right to hire lawyers or sue in Canadian courts. All of this indicates a systematic intent to deliberately wipe out Indian children under the guise of religion and education.

But more than a general de-population was going on in these camps. Particular blood lines of hereditary native leaders were specifically targeted for elimination, as part of the effort to secure control over the lands and resources held by the traditional families.

"I was the daughter of a traditional chief, so I was targeted by the staff for special treatment" described Harriett Nahanee to me when I first met her in Vancouver in December of 1995. "I was raped every night for years. They had me ready for the operation *(ie, sterilization – KA)* but I escaped from there *(Alberni Indian school – KA)* before they could do it. But anyone from my family was either killed or sterilized."

I met another survivor of this west coast eugenics program in the spring of 2004: Campbell Quatell, a descendent of hereditary Kwakiutl chiefs on Vancouver Island, and one of six brothers held in the Anglican residential school in Alert Bay.

"None of us could ever have any children" Campbell told me. "All six of us are sterile. We were put under an X ray machine by those visiting doctors. They held it over my pelvis for a good ten minutes until it started burning me. We were all given a red tag when we arrived at the school once they found out who we were. Anyone who got the red tag got the X rays." (20)

When the Quatell brothers tried suing the government and Anglican church for these damages in 2005, their case was thrown out of court. When they tried accessing their medical records from their years at the Alert Bay school, they were denied them on the grounds that their "treatment" at the school was a "matter of national security". Similar accounts abound from aboriginal survivors of the Nanaimo Indian Hospital, the R.W. Large Hospital in Bella Bella, and eight other sterilization clinics operated by the military and the United Church of Canada, as well as by Indian residential schools across Canada. (21)

The Crown of England and its Anglican church had a special interest in pushing this eugenics program, no doubt because it was the main recipient of the lands gained as a consequence. Anglican missionary and future Indian Agent Harry Guillod commented to his local Bishop in 1894,

"It is proving efficacious to our long term securing of the region to breed out the savages and especially their leaders. The confusion of kinship loyalties and dilution of their bloodlines will go far to extinquishing the Indian identity and solving the Indian problem." (22)

As with the land grabbing, this targeted eugenics carries on today, by the same perpetrating agencies, and for the same reason. In March, 2007 the Community Task Force on Missing Women in Vancouver – the only non-governmental group to do an investigation into these disappearances - stated in its final report,

"The disappearance of our women is neither random nor is it the action of lone killers, but is an organized attack directed against the traditional blue-blood members of the matrilineal Clan Mothers, especially in the northern territories. The Clan Mothers held title to the lands and resources of their people and that knowledge and the ownership of the land passed to the women who are now being hunted and killed ... Considering the blatant cover-up of most of the murders by the RCMP and their involvement in them, and the continued rape of our lands by multinational companies, we are convinced that the disappearances of our women and children are a continuation of the centuries-old genocide of indigenous nations in this province." (23)

Genocide machines are never turned off by those who create them. They only cease when such powers are overthrown and brought to trial in another system of justice. Since such an imposed reckoning has never happened in Canada, where the aboriginal-killing churches, corporations and governments are still firmly in the saddle, native people continue to die: not from the abstracted causes neatly discussed in academic papers and toothless "Royal Commissions", but due to the homicidal plans of men in offices and hit-men on the ground.

The target of these actors is still the land and those who continue to occupy it. And nowhere is this more true and obvious than on Canada's west coast, among the Ahousaht people.

The twentieth century gave birth to the practice and language of concentration camps. Whether in the Boer-confining British facilities in 1900, the Nazi industrial operations, or the church-run "Indian residential schools", such killing grounds were the favoured means of attempting the final death blow against conquered peoples. That changed after World War Two, when the horror of the Nazi years gave genocide an officially bad name and forced its practitioners to become more sophisticated and camouflage their methods.

In Canada, that meant making the co-opted Indian "chiefs" responsible for wiping out the remnants of their own people. This would do away with the need for Indian residential schools and allow the profitable crimes of church, state and business to carry on.

During my years in Port Alberni I ran headlong into this sophisticated neo-colonial arrangement. It was everywhere, and yet its hergemony allowed it to conceal more than it revealed.

Our English word "exterminate" comes from the Latin term *ex-termina* which means "to banish or drive over the border". Populaces who are genocidally targeted are quite literally part of a *Terra Nullius*, a Land of No-One, forced not only from our midst but from our minds. The invisibility of those we've conquered and destroyed allows us to live "guilt-free" alongside the carnage we have caused.

As a pale newcomer to the Alberni Valley, none of the real situation became visible to me until I stepped past the appearances and met the actual survivors of our homegrown death camps in the prisons they still occupied. But first I had to find my way past the prison guards.

"Our own tribal council chiefs are the biggest problem now" Earl George had remarked early in our conversation on that first morning in Bruce Gunn's drafty church building in Ahousaht. "They've been put in charge to keep the rest of us frightened and in line."

That process began years ago, of course, when as children the now-reigning tribal council chiefs were normally the "enforcers" (to use Earl George's term) in the residential schools: spying on, denouncing and disciplining their fellow students at the behest of the church and school staff. The blood of the innocent is on their hands as well, which goes far to explain their fierce opposition to any exposure of criminal actions in the residential schools. As in every neo-colonial divide-and-conquer arrangement, the divisions and warfare among the victims continue today, to benefit the same old interests.

"Why do you think nobody ever challenges those goons?" said Earl George. "We don't forget what they did to us and neither do they. But they got away with their shit then for the same reason they get away with it now, because they're the government's puppets and they're protected."

Under the terms of the so-called treaties between native bands and the federal government, the chiefs' main job these days is twofold: to sign over the last of their lands and resources to state or corporate control and force ever-increasing members of their tribes into poverty and oblivion. Employing the obfuscatory "sustainable development" language of the United Nations, Canada and its client Indian leaders are ensuring that the genocidal agenda is accomplished through the usual legal and seemingly benificent manner, but with the same deadly effect on most surviving Indians.

The template for this extermination was established long

ago. But in terms of the Ahousaht people it began in a turf war between two very different men: a pallid Presbyterian missionary and a traditional, actual indigenous leader. And the consequences of their battle continue to reverberate today.

John Ross *(upper left)*, **Principal of the Ahousaht Indian School, c. 1910**

Our missionary Mr. Ross put them into Jail for two months those four Ahousaht Indians, Mr. Ross is not good teaching for the Childrens he is a Policeman, all over the west coast Indians they know he is Policeman ... Mr. Ross was trouble again with Chief George he was very angry at him and he said he will put Chief George into jail for potlatching and keeping his Childrens out of School.

    - Chief Billy August to Secretary of Indian Affairs, Ottawa, November 25, 1914

For some time I have taken an active part in the suppression of intertribal potlatching. I was the first on the West Coast to lay information before the authorities of a breach of the Indian Act and as a result several of the Indians were sent to jail. Of course there has been trouble between myself and the Ahousaht Tribe ... I have often said, an Indian's loyalty is worth the price of a blanket.

    - Principal John Ross to Department of Indian Affairs, Ottawa, December 24, 1914

In reply I beg to say that Mr. Ross was only acting in the best interests of the Indians and he has been exonerated from all blame in connection with the incident in question.

    - J.D. McLean, Assistant Deputy Secretary of Indian Affairs, Ottawa, to West Coast Indian Agent Charles Cox, March 4, 1915

I regret to enclose the resignation of the Rev. John T. Ross of Ahousaht together with his report of the death of Carrie George, No. 062, daughter of Chief Maquinna George and pupil at the Ahousaht school. Personally I am satisfied that Mr. Ross was in no wise to blame, as the child had evidently procured the matches from her home, as they were of a totally different manufacture to those used in the school.
 - Indian Agent Charles Cox to the Secretary of Indian Affairs, Ottawa, April 6, 1916

It is indeed noteworthy that the land in question, when valued at $15 an acre in 1912, is now being sold by your Church for $200 an acre. This of course is the best part of the property secured originally by your missionaries ...
 - Duncan Campbell Scott, Superintendent General, Department of Indian Affairs, Ottawa, to J.H. Edmison, Secretary of the Presbyerian Church in Canada, concerning Lot 363 at Ahousaht, July 2, 1917

Chapter Four: John Ross versus the Maquinnas

When I first discovered the journals and records of the earliest missionaries among the Ahousaht people, I thought I was reading the notes of land surveyors and real estate speculators.

Rather than matters of the soul or the well being of their aboriginal charges, Presbyterians like John Ross and his predecessor Melvin Swartout, or the Catholic Bishop Auguste Brabant, were obsessed with getting the Indians' land, if one goes by their own accounts.

As the top Methodist official for Home Missions, Alexander Sutherland, implored to the federal government in 1888,

"We have frequently a good deal of trouble with the Indians, growing out of the fact that we have no legal or formal claim to any particular quantity of land. We ask therefore that the Department should give us a title of occupation protecting us alike from complaints of individual Indians or by the band." *(See Figure 7 and Footnote 24)*

Genocide is ultimately about theft, whether of another peoples' home land, their identity, or their lives. The west coast missionaries of every denomination were not the only ones who were explicit about this goal. As their faithful handmaiden, the federal and provincial governments of Canada entrenched the corporate and land-grabbing nature and power of these churches in the founding charters that legally permitted the churches' invasion and conquest of non-Christian nations. That assault was officially authorized from its inception.

Foremost in this regard was the United Church of Canada, which was formed by an Act of Parliament in July, 1924 to amalgamate the Presbyterian and Methodist churches and more effectively "Canadianize and Christianize" the Indians. **That Act placed the United Church outside the laws of Canada and granted it the powers of a court and a bank.** The Church as a "Body Corporate" could lend and borrow money, purchase, lease and convey land and property, make and execute promissory notes and bills of exchange, and have the power to collect on loans and enforce its own legal judgments.

What was equally astounding was the fact that any Canadian laws that were at odds with the United Church of Canada Act were "hereby repealed" by that Act. In short, the major Canadian Protestant missionary church, like the Roman Catholic Church, had been made into a law and a power unto itself by the Canadian government and its sponsor in London. *(See Footnote 12)*

As a self-governing corporation unaccountable for its actions under Canadian law, the United Church, alongside the Catholics and the Anglicans, was created to lead the assault on the remnant aboriginal nations. It did so not only by operating the main Protestant Indian residential schools but the Indian Hospitals across British Columbia, where generations of children were sterilized and experimented upon by church and military doctors. *(see www.murderbydecree.com)* But the Church's earliest goal was to consolidate the land grabs of its antecedent Presbyterian missionaries like John Ross and profit from the Indian schools they'd inherited: in Ahousaht, Port Alberni, and all over British Columbia.

One of the reasons the United Church was able to do so with such effectiveness and concealment was because of the earlier brutality deployed by John Ross and his counterparts against the Ahousahts and other coastal nations.

Upon arriving in Ahousaht in the spring of 1904, John Ross began constructing an Indian boarding school. To ensure the attendance therein, Ross appointed special "native constables" to round up and incarcerate nearly all of the Ahousaht children. In January 1910 Ross was appointed Principal of the school. In many cases, he personally arrested those Ahousahts who were holding their traditional potlatch ceremonies. Until his sudden resignation in April of 1916, John Ross ruled many of the Ahousahts with an iron hand, targeting especially those traditional elders like Chiefs Maquinna George and Billy August who opposed Ross.

Such draconian power by coastal missionaries was not unique to John Ross or the Presbyterians, but was generally required by all the churches because of the continued independence and resistance of the Ahousahts and their neighbors. As noted, an Indian Affairs memorandum dated December 18,

1902 lamented that only two of the 273 registered Ahousaht Indians were Christians, and that in the entire region over half of the Indians remained "Pagan". *(Figure 1)* In that same period (1901), Presbyterians "owned" barely a third of the converted Indians, which gave that church a particular conquering-zeal. *(See Figure 8)*

And so as the 20th century dawned, the defiant Ahousahts became the chief target of state-backed missionaries on Canada's west coast: especially the Presbyterian late-comers. By 1910, the central west coast of Vancouver Island held more Indian boarding and day schools than any other part of Canada.

John Ross was a particular zealot, even by Christian missionary standards. During 1903 he had arranged his assignment to the Ahousahts after hearing that the then-serving Presbyterian missionary, John Russell, was unsuccessful in his efforts to bring Ahousaht children into a day school he'd operated among them since 1901. In Ross' words, penned retrospectively on Christmas eve of 1914, "For some time I have taken an active part in the suppression of intertribal potlatching. I was the first on the West Coast to lay information before the authorities of a breach of the Indian Act in regard to the custom ... the intertribal potlatching custom is bad. So long as it continues there is no possibility of Indian advancement in British Columbia. Of course, naturally, the Indian feels pretty sore about the new law and they were angry because I was the first to take up a case ..." *(See Figure 9)*

What John Ross leaves out is who exactly he brought charges against for doing the potlatching: namely, the two hereditary elders of the Ahousahts, Chief Maquinna George and his brother, Chief Billy August. Both brothers resisted Ross, kept their children out of the Indian boarding school he'd established, and wrote petitions against Ross to the federal government. As early as November 1904, the same year Ross' boarding school opened, one of these protests referred to Ross:

".... it was four altogether go to Jail Mrs. Billy August, Chief Johnny Charlie, Sam, fred gillet of kilsomaths Indian, our Missionary Mr. Ross to do so, put them into Jail those four

Ahousat Indians. Mr. Ross is not good teaching for the Childrens, he is Policeman ... Mr. Ross always make lots of trouble ..." *(See Figure 10)*

Chief Billy August, author of this letter to the government, never received a reply. But within two years of his first opposition to John Ross, all four of Chief Billy's children were dead. One of them, Will, was poisoned while in John Ross' care at the Ahousaht school. And some years later, Chief Maquinna George's only daughter Carrie also died in the school, having been burned to death. Then, the following week, John Ross hurriedly resigned as Principal and left the area after having been exonerated of any wrongdoing in Carrie's death by the district Indian Agent. *(See Figure 11)*

As the passing of time revealed, there was another purpose behind John Ross' pit-bull assault on the traditional Ahousaht leaders and their families: namely, to secure all of the latter's land by wiping out their hereditary blood lines. This tried and true genocidal method of stealing indigenous land is still employed today by resource-hungry companies and their business partners in the RCMP, churches and government. (25)

The effectiveness of this method can be measured through the close correlation between the eradication of traditional chiefly families and the loss of indigenous territories in any given area. This method was tried and perfected by missionaries like John Ross, especially those within the Presbyterian-United Church tradition, which alongside the Anglicans, represented the Anglo-Saxon cultural mainstream of Canada's Scots-English ruling class during the 19th and 20th centuries.

One of the clues behind Ross' land grabbing agenda was his close association with the earliest Presbyterian missionary to the west coast, Melvin Swartout, and with the Anglican missionary *cum* land speculator *cum* Indian Agent, Harry Guillod.

Originally a school teacher, Swartout was ordained quite rapidly and then sent out among the Ohiat Indians at Ucluelet, south of Ahousaht, in the fall of 1891. But most of his early years there Swartout spent mapping the coastal islands and surveying the lands claimed by the Ohiats. In these efforts he was aided by Harry Guillod, who shielded

Swartout from the opposition of the local Catholic Bishop August Brabant. Guillod had an obvious economic motive in helping Swartout, since Guillod was operating his own sawmill near Port Alberni and personally profited off Swartout's land surveys, especially of the cedar-rich lands among the still-independent Ohiat Indian band in Barclay Sound. *(See Figure 12)*

Melvin Swartout worked closely with John Ross after the latter appeared on the coast in 1903. With his help and Harry Guillod's protection, Swartout effectively mapped the entire coast of central Vancouver island and its vast timber resources while planting church missions among the Indians like the Ohiats who held those same resources. The Ahousaht oral history, shared with the author by Chief Earl George and Nelson Keithlah, describes the two Presbyterian missionaries as "men hungry for our land", to quote Earl George. "They stayed just long enough to steal something. No wonder my grandfather hated them so much."

That hatred by Earl's grandfather, Chief Billy August, possibly displayed itself in more than irate petitions. On July 10, 1904,

Swartout's dead body was found tangled in kelp off the Ahousahts' coastline. Unusually, the local Indian Agents including Harry Guillod conducted no public investigation and buried the story of Swartout's death; nor did the Presbyterian Church pursue the matter.

Considering the land speculating and profiteering conducted by church and state, Swartout's surveying activities were no doubt something meant to remain hidden by those institutions. A veil of secrecy descended on the history of Swartout, Ross and the eventual inside land-deal between the Presbyterians / United Church and their corporate associates. But what is certain is that Swartout's death coincided with the launching of the dozen year turf war between the Maquinnas and John Ross. That struggle ended briefly with the latter's sudden departure from Ahousaht under a cloud of suspicion after Carrie George's violent death. But in 1917, after the Ahousahts burned the boarding school to the ground, John Ross returned to construct a new building. At the time a church report stated, "It is supposed that the Indian children burned the school. The mentality of the Indians is very low and possibly a different type of discipline or more frequent vacations would have avoided such an incident." (26)

Ross in fact did more than rebuild the Indian school. The same year, in the fall of 1917, he convinced his Presbyterian church to sell to the government the land on which the school stood, adjacent to the main Ahousaht village of Maaqtusiis. Soon a top Presbyterian official wrote to Ottawa making the offer. To the church, "saving the savages" apparently took second place to making some big bucks.

Having seized the land outright without compensating the Ahousahts by a single penny, the Presbyterians stood to make a bundle on the plot of land, which was later designated as Lot 363. J.H. Edmison for the church's Home Missions Board offered ten acres of the land to the federal government at $200 an acre – a price exorbitantly inflated from the $15 an acre it was assessed at only five years earlier. The government turned them down. *(See Figure 13)*

No doubt chagrined, John Ross left Ahousaht for good shortly after the failed land sale, although he settled not far away. Ross was soon appointed as a teacher at the Ucluelet Indian day school, established years before by his deceased associate Melvin Swartout. Clearly, the missionary didn't want to let go of a good thing.

Sure enough, in 1953 his own grandson Hamilton Ross acquired all of Lot 363 from the then-United Church of Canada for a mere $2000, or $10 an acre, about one twentieth of its value by that time, and far below the price the church had asked for it when it tried selling the land to the Canadian government in 1917. Hamilton Ross then flipped and sold the land to the United Church's corporate benefactor MacMillan-Bloedel, the largest west coast logging company, for $6000: a quick profit for Ross and a huge deal for Mac-Blo. (27) Clearly, swindling Indians seemed to run in the family.

Thanks to John Ross and his church and state backers, the traditional Ahousahts were eradicated during those subsequent years, as they were meant to be. Under the blows of germ warfare and the residential schools genocide, not only did their numbers fall to below 200 people but their traditional leaders like the Maquinnas were ravaged and politically sidelined. In their place the government established transplanted convert-puppets like the Edgar, Frank and Atleo families, who became the state-run "Ahousaht tribal council" chiefs and who still rule the roost in Ahousaht.

And so, as on every Indian reservation across Canada, two distinct aboriginal societies came into being among Chief Earl George's people: an "official" one funded and run from Ottawa, and a submerged and beseiged traditional one, of which Earl was one of the few surviving remnants. And one day Earl would show to me and to the world how some of the substance of his obstinate warrior-ancestors had endured.

Interlude: All in the Family

As this school was the property of, and conducted by, the Church, care was taken to avoid too close (an) inquiry.
> - Indian Agent P. D. Ashbridge, reporting on a fire and related wrongdoing at the Ahousaht Indian Residential School, January 26, 1940 *(See Figure 14)*

Come now Kevin, you don't believe there's a separation of church and state in this country, do you?
> - B.C. Conflict of Interest Commissioner H.D. Oliver to the author, March 14, 1999

Under a regime where mass murder is officially sanctioned, there can be no regret and no apology.
> - Simon Wisenthal, <u>Justice not Vengence</u>

History bears out the simple fact that Genocide is not a crime but a normative tool of Church and State. As such, it is rarely prosecuted, and only by the victors of a war against the defeated. When genocidal acts are put on trial, the charges are made against scapegoated individuals and not the regimes or ideologies that caused the slaughter. For like war itself, Genocide is not meant to be stopped.

I only began to understand this fact after living for awhile in the ashes of the Ahousaht nation and among men with blood on their hands. The ones who had warehoused and tortured to death the Ahousaht children and then buried their remains in the depth of night were still alive and secure when I arrived in Port Alberni in 1992. Some of them still are. And never over the years did any of them express a genuine look or a word of remorse for what they and their churches did to legions of the innocent.

Simon Wiesenthal was right. When official society commits and condones mass murder, it becomes not a crime but an arrangement to be accommodated and safeguarded. The moment I asked the United Church why it stole the Ahousahts' land and killed their children, I became an outsider. First the Church and then the State closed ranks against me to defend their everyday genocide and its profits. Then my real education began.

Harry Truman wisely observed, "The only thing that's new

under the sun is the history you didn't know about." The bloody debris of home grown crimes that we stumble over has never been that hidden; it only seems concealed to us because our own eyes are firmly shut to what is in our midst. And so the issue is never one of a lack of evidence but of our own myopia, and our will to disbelieve.

A retired Royal Engineer and colonial businessman named Francis Poole wrote these words shortly before his death in 1873:

"In the summer of 1862 and in the manner of our Anglican colleagues, I led the party that introduced contagious smallpox among the Indians in Bella Coola and Fort Alexander. We acted on behalf of Attorney General George Carey and our fellow New Aberdeen Land Company shareholders. We were successful. Nearly all of the savages died." (28)

Poole and his group destroyed the Nuxalk people with germ warfare in a few short months by reducing their population from over 4000 to "a few dozen". He had previously laid a claim to all of the Nuxalk land in the Colonial Land Office in New Westminster in the usual "pre-empt, then slaughter" pattern of priests like Anglican missionary John Sheepshanks and other agents of the Octopus: the three-headed beast of Church, State and Business that grabbed the west coast.

The Octopus was and continues to be one extended family. Its members have traditionally been linked by marriage and kinship bonds, and its depredations blessed and legitimated by the Church of England, usually in conjunction with the Scots-Presbyterians and the Church of Rome. Its conquests were profit-driven and carved up into jurisdictions overseen by the different churches.

Since the Ahousahts fell under the control of the Presbyterians and later the United Church of Canada, so did the richest stands of old growth red cedar in western Vancouver Island. And as the creation and insider-partner of the federal government, the United Church was ideally placed to facilitate the biggest multinational corporate land grab in British Columbia history during the 1990's, against the Tom Thumb opposition of Earl George and myself.

As we've seen with Harry Guillod, John Ross and other early missionaries, the members of the Octopus have traditionally performed interchangeable roles, moving freely between church, government and the corporate world. In practice, there is no separation of church and state and big money. Mirroring the British aristocracy, where one family's sons would often include an Army General, a Banker, a High Church Bishop or a House of Lords Peer, the Octopus sees its purpose as divinely ordained, above the law, morality and any accountability. The Octopus is in fact the law.

Despite its present garbing in the outward ornaments of formal "democracy", Canada continues to operate according to the in-house norms of this exclusive club. This became transparently clear to me the more I rubbed the United Church the wrong way by inadvertantly exposing the close ties between its top officers, the provincial government, foreign multinational companies and the ever-compliant tribal council "chiefs" of the west coast.

The details of how I discovered all this, and went up against their arrangement, are laid out in the next chapter. What I revealed was nothing less than the way our culture actually operates: a very old arrangement that we call western civilization, in whose gory normalities we dwell and which we buttress every day. So it bears reminding ourselves how that cozy "All in the Family" set up laid the basis for the continued Group Crime of which the Lot 363 deal is one example.

In this regard, two dates stand out in the history of this crime: April 12, 1876 and July 1, 1920. On both days, a small group of self-governing, wealthy Englishmen met "In Council" in Ottawa and passed two genocidal laws: the Indian Act of Canada and An Act to Establish Industrial Schools for Indians. These "Order in Council" statutes were never authorized nor debated by the Canadian Parliament or within courts of law. The Indians affected by these Acts, of course, had no say in the matter.

Despite the obfuscating language of these in-house statutes, their murderous aims and consequences are apparent. But what is less obvious is the identity of the men who promulgated them. In truth, they were all from the same class and aristocratic in-group, either by birth or favoured appointment. No doubt this was one of the reasons that these "laws" were enacted in the name of one of their close friends: a super-wealthy foreign autocrat on a gilded throne in London.

The Indian Act of 1876 created the general framework for legal genocide in Canada; the Industrial Schools Act of 1920 was the finishing touch on that effort. Between these two dates – and keep that significant half-century period in mind for a moment – occured the decisive land grab and final extermination of west coast native nations, led by the Church of Rome and of England, and by the United Church's predecessors, the Presbyterians.

The Canadian Genocide was originally a Roman invention that lay at the heart of all European theory and practice of religious conquest. Because of this, when the Vatican became politically eclipsed in 1870 by Giuseppe Garibaldi's annullment of the Papal States, the government of Canada and its master in London were compelled to intervene on behalf of Rome to sustain their joint project of pagan conquest. This was part of the geo-political cause of the Acts of 1876 and 1920.

In the same manner, when the Vatican was restored to political status by the dictator Mussolini in 1929, and established its in-house policy of covering up its own crimes known as *Crimen Sollicitationas,* in that same year the government of Canada relinquished legal control of the Indian residential schools to the (predominantly Catholic) churches that ran them. This tag-team responsibility for the crime, and the mutual dependency between church and state, was so normative that the two institutions should not be considered as separate actors.

In justifying the Indian Act, Prime Minister Alexander MacKenzie declared "The great aim of our legislation has been to do away with the tribal system and assimilate the Indian people in all respects." It was no accident that in describing Indian Policy he chose the Latin word "assimilate" or "ad similis", meaning "to be like": *to ingest and incorporate something and turn it into its host.* Indeed, this Roman-Papal belief in eating The Other and making it a part of itself imbued every level of western politics, law and religion. (29)

In the mind of the Conqueror-Eater, its extermination of the

Other is an act of benevolence, of raising non-existing Non-Persons into real, although enslaved and subordinate, beings that are "incorporated" into and made part of a bigger body, or "corpus" (corpse). This of course is a very old Roman idea that later acquired Christian terminology and trappings.

Under Roman Law, foreign lands and peoples targeted for conquest became "Nullus", considered empty of people and therefore open for seizure. Foreigners in the crosshairs of Rome therefore ceased to exist, just as Roman popes later declared the lands of non-Catholics to be *Terra Nullius* – "The Land of No-One" – that could be absorbed into the papal Corpus. The invisible Others could be given a conditional and limited humanity by their baptism and enslavement, a process, significantly, termed "reconciliation" by church lawyers. Those who resisted were required to be exterminated.

What's more, to the Papacy this process of conquest not only elevated the surviving Others from a state of non-being into semi-humanity, but it morally perfected the conqueror as well, thanks to the convenient 11th century, Crusading doctrine of Indulgence. The latter, enunciated by Pope Urban, declared that any Catholic who waged war against enemies of the church was "returned to a state of original grace", freed of all sins and wrongdoing. Genocide, in short, was a good and moral thing for both the victim and the perpetrator: an actual spiritual cleansing, or "Act of Faith", (*auto da fe*) as the papacy referred to its Inquisitional torture and killing of dissident Others. (30)

This culture of Benevolent Butchery, of absorbing an element of a conquered people into a Body Politic, was part of the mental armour worn by the same missionaries and land grabbers who killed off the Ahousahts and other coastal nations. It continues to be carried by the Invaders' descendents, including by the so-called liberal element of White Canada. When I was summarily cashiered from my United Church pulpit in early 1995 for unveiling some of our in-house crimes, the chairman of my church board, Fred Bishop, announced that my biggest offense had been to "upset the life of our Church Family". The Octopus doesn't deal well with strangers or unpleasant reminders.

Canada was constructed as an ideal colonial Family Arrangement, and it remains so today. Prior to Confederation, its predominant English aristocracy in Upper Canada was collectively known as The Family Compact: a coterie of inter-married Anglican Bishops, bankers and businessmen who ruled the country through Executive Order and "noblesse oblige". The British Crown allowed a parallel hierarchy to exist next door in Quebec, managed by the Bishops of the Church of Rome and francophone civil servants.

Anyone who challenged this cozy arrangement ended up at the end of a rope or exiled to Australia, as happened to the Republican rebels of 1837. And after the crushing of these Patriots' aborted democratic uprising, the Crown cemented a Church-State oligarchy into place that not only stripped Euro-Canadians of any form of accountable government but was directly responsible for the ensuing aboriginal genocide across the nation. (31)

Besides the stifling political climate of such a closed, hierarchical regime, the psychological effect of this arrangement on pale Canadians has been even more profound, akin to Aristotle's elitist belief that "Power cannot be devoid of virtue": that is, all Might is not only Right, but Upright. To this day, most Anglo-Canadians cannot accept that their churches and governments deliberately set out to kill off most of the country's Indians. It all had to be an accident of some kind, or "a well intentioned plan gone awry", to quote John Milloy of Trent University, one of Canada's more odious establishment academicians.

Such an obtuse mentality not only places the hard evidence and renegade Canadians like me outside the Pale of their national corpus, but compels a vast industry of historical make-believe and self-exculpation that would make even a hardened spin doctor cringe.

Unlike the general climate south of our border, Canadians genuinely tend to respect and fear authority, whether it be secular or religious. The rapidity with which my former stalwart friends and congregants literally scurried to avoid me after my firing and blacklisting by the United Church was an ample lesson of this fact. But this Great Fear by Canadians of the club-wielding angry parent has also allowed the crimes of the Octopus to carry on as before, with a few tinkered modifications to placate the anxious child-citizens – those pliant "subjects of the Crown" – who desperately seek the virtue in their Masters.

Perhaps eyewitness Harriett Nahanee's observation to me one night shortly after we met was an accurate diagnosis about my people as well as her own: that the only ones to survive the genocide were "slaves and sellouts". Nevertheless, some of the crowd on the Imperial Menu are occasionally tossed aside by the Octopus as undigestible bits; and rather than fade away, these remnant ones actually place a stone in their slings in the face of the Goliath of corporatized Church and State.

It happened to Harriett, and to me.

One does not sell the earth upon which the people walk.
      - Chief Seattle

As the Ha-wilth for Ahousat Nation I am requesting the Province to stop this interference in our proposed negotiations in order to peacefully come to a just settlement for all territories known to all Nuu-chah-nulth First Nations.

> - Letter of Chief Earl Maquinna George to B.C. Government, November 16, 1992, in reference to his reclaiming of all of Lot 363 for his people

The very fact that we are waiting for the Ahousats to prove their case to us, or to meet with us on our terms, indicates a perpetuation of the racist and oppressive relationship that has been our legacy regarding indigenous peoples ... If we do not clearly and publicly admit our wrong on this matter, and seek actively to return the land in question to the Ahousats people, I will find it difficult to associate myself with the United Church on this issue.

> - Letter of Rev. Kevin Annett to the Comox-Nanaimo Presbytery, United Church of Canada, October 17, 1994, just prior to his firing without cause

The collusion of church, state and multinational business officials in the take over and exploitation of native land resources, specifically Lot 363, and the attempt to silence Chief George and Rev. Annett, constitute a violation of both hereditary land claims and basic human rights.

> \- Ahousahts' clergyman Rev. Bruce Gunn to the World Council of Churches, Geneva, January 15, 1997

Chapter Five:

Showdown on the Coast –

A Tale of Two Letters and A Takeover

The old Ahousaht man and I occupied two very different worlds, but soon after my arrival on his land our tangents began to cross. Perhaps the cruelly indifferent hand of Fate was the cause, or maybe it was the inevitable outcome of a crime too long hidden. But soon after Earl George and Bruce Gunn and I first sat over tea in the drafty cold of Bruce's Ahousaht church building, and I learned the story of Earl's people and the land called Lot 363, some explosive ingredient between us began to simmer and boil.

On the rainy spring day in 1993 when Earl and I made our acquaintance, he was already waist-deep in conflict with a host of powerful enemies: the provincial New Democratic Party government, the United Church of Canada, his own profit-hungry fellow band council chiefs, and the big money behind them all, MacMillan-Bloedel and its partner Weyerhauser Ltd.: the biggest logging company in the world. All of these forces wanted Earl George out of the way.

Earl was a marked man by this Juggernaut for a simple reason: the previous autumn in a letter to the provincial government, Earl had publicly claimed all of the cedar-rich Lot 363 for his people. It was his role as traditional Keeper of the Land to do exactly that. The land was not to be logged, said Earl. Money came second to the purpose given to him and to his people by the Creator and their own laws.

Of these four opponents, the United Church stood to lose the most in the way of credibility and public image if Earl got his way.

For one thing, the century-old secret would be out of the bag. The church would be exposed as a speculator in stolen native land, where many native children had died at church hands in the Ahousaht residential school. As well, the church would be seen to be guilty of the worst kind of double-dealing and hypocrisy: for after Earl had written his land claim letter the previous November, the United Church had completely reversed its previous sponsorship of Earl as the first west coast aboriginal candidacy for United Church ministry. Suddenly, no money could be found in the church's coffers for Earl's candidacy, even though he had been promised a $6000 grant by the church just before he wrote his letter that had inconveniently named the same United Church as responsible for the original theft of Lot 363.

None of Earl's urgent letters and phone calls to the church officers were ever answered. Instead, a standard black ops, gossip and smear campaign began against him among the Ahousaht people, fed by the church's buddies on the band council. The sixty seven year old Indian began to visibly crack under the strain.

Naturally, all of these stabs in the back had made Earl and Bruce livid, but Bruce urged caution. He was somewhat naively trying to convince the church to keep Earl on board. Bruce showed me a ream of diplomatically polite but firm letters he had written to Ed Searcy, head of the United Church's Land Claims Committee, who had taken the original initiative to sponsor Earl for ministry. Bruce wanted an explanation why Earl was now getting sidelined. But as a loyal church appartchik, Searcy played dumb and referred Bruce back to his own Presbytery, and to other bovine officials who feigned the same know-nothing, do-nothing attitude.

And so the rhetorical rodeo carried on.

At the same time, and in typical tag-team fashion, the other members of the Octopus started ganging up on Earl in a manner identical to what they would inflict on me and my family barely two years later, after I had objected in writing to the covert theft of Lot 363. Earl was suddenly excluded from band council meetings by the other "chiefs" and never informed of their decisions. Similarly, the NDP government's land claims negotiators ignored Earl entirely and went around him, dealing instead with the sellout band councillors to secure the land for Weyerhauser. This brazen insult to the Ahousaht's chief spiritual elder was entirely calculated, and engineered by Earl's own colleagues. Meanwhile, the United Church paid a direct bribe of $14,000 to the sellout chiefs during this same period, according to a letter issued by Bruce Gunn in 1999. *(See Figure 15)*

As it turned out, Earl was sitting on a bigger political powder keg than he or any of us realized at the time. What was in the works was nothing less than the incorporation of the coastal native nations as business partners into the multinational corporate takeover and eradication of the last old growth rain forests on Vancouver Island.

Unknown to Earl, every individual Ahousaht band was being offered an initial $500,000 in government handouts by signing on to what was known as the Provincial Interim Measures Agreement (PIMA). The latter was the single master contract that oversaw the carving up of the old growth forests by foreign companies and their aboriginal junior business partners. But of course the biggest winners were Weyerhauser and the B.C. Government. The latter had recently become the biggest share holder in the company that Weyerhauser was about to buy up, MacMillan-Bloedel, which owned most of the tree farm licenses on Vancouver Island. (32)

By his intransigent opposition to the sale of Lot 363, Earl George was suddenly the proverbial spoke in the wheel, since the PIMA could not be signed and the big bucks couldn't start flowing until all local land claims had been settled. And PIMA had a deadline – December 31, 1993 – after which all deals were off. But by May, when we first talked, Earl George was still saying no. And so not surprisingly, panic was beginning to spread in the boardrooms, church and band council offices, which no doubt explains the strong-arm tactics the Gang of Four started using against Earl.

The "owner" of the forests at the time, MacMillan-Bloedel Ltd., ("Mac-Blo") had had a long financial relationship with the United Church of Canada. Its founder, H.R. MacMillan (1885-1976) had been the head of the first logging brokerage firm in British Columbia, a member of the British elite and a patron of the United Church, establishing the MacMillan Family Endowment that still funds United Churches and seminaries. In fact, soon after the Lot 363 deal was finally secured, the MacMillan Fund granted the biggest bequest in its history to First United Church in Port Alberni: the home church of Jan Schlackl, a Mac-Blo company director who had helped arrange Earl George's sidelining and my firing from the next door United Church. (33)

An even more prominent United Church actor in this whole sordid mess was the provincial Aboriginal Affairs Minister at the time, United Church clergyman John Cashore, who wore the usual colonial two-hats of church and state. All during this period, Reverend Cashore used his NDP government office to secretly facilitate the acquisition of Lot 363 by MacMillan-Bloedel (that is, by its standing-in-the-wings new owner, Weyerhauser) while arranging to exclude his own United Church from all land negotiations so as not to expose their role in originally stealing the land.

According to Ahousaht clergyman Bruce Gunn, who watched the Lot 363 debacle from up close,

"There's no question that John Cashore tried to run interference for the church and sidetrack the church connection to the land deal using government money, as early as the spring of 1994. Cashore's role became pretty blatant long before your removal. At an August, 1994 meeting in Ahousaht set up to resolve the Lot 363 land deal issue, I objected to the government mediator ... that the United Church wasn't present, when they had owned and sold Lot 363. I asked him if their absence was related to the fact that the Aboriginal Affairs minister was also a United Church minister. The mediator said later that he wasn't aware about the church's role in it at all, because he was 'under instructions not to include the church in negotiations.' ". *(From a phone conversation to the author from Bruce Gunn in March 1999. See Figure 15)*

John Cashore also took a personal role in torpedoing both Earl and me, as he declared to the Comox-Nanaimo Presbytery official Win Stokes just prior to my firing without cause when he declared,

"We can't have Kevin upset the applecart over Lot 363. There's too much at stake." (34)

Cashore was less indirect when it came to Earl. At a United Church gathering in the summer of 1993, when Earl was still refusing to agree to the Lot 363 sale, Cashore approached him with a cold smile and said,

"Earl, you don't really think you're ever going to become a

United Church minister, do you?" (35)

As it turns out, the growing pressure on Earl had its desired effect. Before the end of the year, Earl caved in. Through some unstated combination of bribery, threats and a sudden heart attack he suffered in November, Earl George finally agreed to the Lot 363 deal. His name appeared at the top of the final PIMA agreement, dated December 10, 1993.

Unfortunately, signing the PIMA didn't relieve the pressure on Earl one bit. He remained a permanent outcast among the other Ahoushat chiefs, who in tandem with MacMillan-Blodel quickly established their own Joint Venture company, Lisaak Ltd., to begin logging off the venerable ancient trees on Lot 363. Similarly, and without explanation, the United Church continued to deny Earl any funding for his training for the ministry.

In response, and no doubt feeling betrayed once more, Earl threatened to go public and tell all by the early months of 1994. At that point he was paid a visit at his home in Ahousaht by two United Church officials – Cameron Reid and

Bill Howie – who would later that year arrange my secret firing from my Port Alberni church. Earl never disclosed what they said to him but after that day he never spoke of the Lot 363 fiasco ever again. A few years later he died of unspecified causes, still isolated and publicly disparaged by the bought and paid for Ahousaht chiefs.

Unfortunately for the prematurely-jubilant United Church and the other land-profiteers in their Gang of Four, later in that same year I picked up the torch that Earl had dropped. It all began for me at an otherwise banal gathering of fellow United Church clergy at our Comox-Nanaimo Presbytery meeting in Gold River, B.C. on a miserably cold weekend in October of 1994.

I had been ensconced as the minister at St. Andrew's United Church for over two years by then, and I felt secure. Despite a rump of Old Guard oppositionists who hated me for bringing Indians into "their" church, thanks to all my labors my congregation had grown from a dozen to over eighty regular Sunday participants. That same month of October, 1994, at a special congregational meeting, my work in ministry had been endorsed by my parishioners by a vote of 54 to 6. I had received only accolades from local United Church officials up to then. Even the senior church personnel officer who removed me from my pulpit, Art Anderson, later admitted,

"Kevin's ministry was admirable, impeccable and above reproach. We had no concerns about him until he wrote that letter about Lot 363". (36)

But amidst my false and facile optimism, the shoe suddenly dropped.

I was sitting in relative boredom during the last day of the Gold River Presbytery gathering when the minister who had first shown me around Port Alberni, Oliver Howard, stood up and told a whopping lie about the Ahousahts. Besides being my pastor-predecessor at St. Andrew's United Church, Oliver had also been part of the United Church's slam-dunk team against Earl George over the previous two years, refusing to meet with Earl or explain why his seminary funding had been squashed. And to add to the injury Howard stood up at the Prebytery meeting that weekend and declared to the delegates,

"None of the Ahousahts want to meet with us about Lot 363. We've tried but they refuse. And they're claiming the land was always theirs but they have no paperwork to prove it. So I see no reason to worry about this thing any longer."

Everything Oliver said was bullshit, as I knew from my own personal experience and discussions with Earl and other Ahousaht members. It was the church that was stonewalling, and denying the existence of the correspondence from 1904 that proved that the Prebsyterian missionaries Melvin Swartout and John Ross had stolen Lot 363 and other nearby land without offering the Ahousahts a penny for it. And so in the vapid company of my fellow clergymen, I was witnessing the concealment that follows any crime. And I knew that I would be an accessory to that felony if I remained silent.

I still can't say exactly why I wrote the subsequent letter to the Presbytery that sealed my fate. Neither Earl George nor Bruce Gunn were there to urge me on. I know that I felt a visceral disgust with the sham I was part of, and that I had to say so. I also know that I acted on impulse and didn't give a thought to the consequences of challenging the church over Lot 363. I was supremely naive at the time, and perhaps willfully ignorant of what I was part of. I genuinely believed that if a wrong was pointed out, the United Church would do what was right – and stand by its own governing policy on native land claims, which was to freely return all aboriginal land in its possession to its original owners.

I quoted that policy when I sat down that night and wrote a single page letter to the Presbytery's Executive and members. I pointed out that we had not returned to the Ahousahts land we had taken from them, and that we were hiding our wrong behind obfuscation and untruths. I asked them to consider the damage our church would suffer if such duplicity was made public. My concern was for our institutional integrity and for the Ahousahts. I wrote without rancor but said I couldn't be associated with land theft and moral irresponsibility. I assumed that I would be listened to. I never imagined what my words would unleash. *(See a copy of my letter in Figure 16)*

My letter was never answered. But later that week, unknown to me, two senior Presbytery officials came to Port Alberni and met secretly with the few members of my congregation who were hostile to me. A coup was being planned.

It took the few church officials who organized my downfall two more months to achieve it, using the same methods they had deployed against Earl George and that their kind still use: rumor, innuendo, lies and fear-mongering. It took that long because I was a very popular minister, beloved by many in my congregation and in town. But I was equally hated by a rump of church members who were personally tied to the residential school crimes – the same six who had voted against me at our October, 1994 church gathering. Ignoring once again due process and the church's governing policy, Art Anderson, Bill Howie, Cameron Reid and Jon Jessiman sided with this small faction to have me ousted from my pulpit and eventually expelled from my profession and livelihood.

When it happened, the coup was planned for maximum destruction, which is the way of desperate men with much to lose. My wife Anne McNamee and I were called in front of Anderson and Reid on January 23, 1995, and I was presented with an ultimatum. Either I would agree to an immediate psychiatric evaluation and a year of unpaid "pastoral retraining", or I would lose my position as minister and likely my ordination. They were about to tear up my family's meal ticket unless I cooperated in their crime. I was given forty eight hours to respond to their demand in writing. The two of them left me in shock and Anne in tears.

I never agreed to their dictate, but my refusal cost me my marriage, my livelihood and my children. But even in the midst of their thuggery, my adversaries let slip their unstated aims. For the first question their church-appointed psychiatrist was to ask me was this: "Why did you write that letter about the Lot 363 land acquisition?"

If challenging one's employer for their own misdeeds qualifies one for psychiatric examination, then in the eyes of my Inquisitors I had already been tried and found guilty – like any opponent of the church. Like any intransigent Ahousaht, I had been assigned to the status of a savage, a Nullus, a non-being against whom any amount of force was legally and morally justified, and permitted. Indeed, in the ensuing tragic months that became years, I learned up close how the church was not simply a law unto itself but an unrestrained force of destruction, blithely encouraged and sanctioned by the willing collusion of the courts, the RCMP, the government, and all of "respectable" Canadian society.

And thus did I see that, if the church would shred to pieces one of their own clergymen and his family simply for questioning their deeds, imagine what they did to those Others of darkened hue and darker unbelief who dared to stand in their way?

Of course they killed them. And of course they killed their children.

....

Like all aftermaths, the outcome to our Tale of Two Letters was perhaps too predictable. The bad guys got their way, since money and history were on their side.

But things didn't stop there. Early in 1997, Bruce Gunn and I issued a public appeal and petition to the World Council of Churches (WCC) and the media that laid out the entire scandal, including the deceitful behaviour of the United Church.

Our appeal called for reparations and a public inquiry. It was never answered by the WCC, nor did the media respond, but our effort sealed the fate of both Bruce and me within church circles. *(See the Petition in Figure 17)*

Our battle entered a brief hiatus after that. Earl George folded up and passed on, and Bruce Gunn soon retired under pressure from the United Church and after his wife, too, left him. But I did the opposite, continuing to be more than a thorn in the side of the Octopus.

The same year that Weyerhauser finally gobbled up MacMillan-Bloedel, in the summer of 1999, a news commentator looked over my evidence and wondered in print how it was that an ostensibly anti-corporatist party like the New Democrats had while the government faciliated the buying up of the province's largest company, MacMillan-Bloedel, by a foreign multinational like Weyerhauser.

"Suddenly it's the NDP defending globalization" declared Vaughan Palmer in his June 22, 1999 column in the *Vancouver Sun*.

"The NDP had a lot to do with making MacBlo ripe for takeover by reducing the harvest rate, increasing production costs and lowering the profits of the forest sector ... The changes have knocked $3 billion off the value of corporate assets ... So you can see the results of the NDP's handiwork in the fate of the largest company of them all, put through the wringer and now delivered, giftwrapped by the NDP into the hands of the Americans." *(See the article in Figure 18)*

Follow the money, indeed. And as we've seen, the money has always been about the land and how to get it. Every missionary, banker and Indian Agent has always known that, especially on Canada's west coast. I had to learn it the hard way.

Still clinging to vestiges of outraged naivety despite years of battling church and state, during 2001 I lodged a formal complaint against John Cashore with the Provincial "Conflict of Interest Commissioner": a portly old gentleman named H.D. Oliver. He seemed more than amused as he listened to me with a retiring smugness across the ornate table in his downtown high rise office.

After considering my complaint that Cashore had used his governmental office to protect his own United Church from scandal and facilitate a backroom land grab from which he personally profited, Mr. Oliver smiled and dropped the comment that he, too, was a "loyal church member".

Seeing that I still hadn't caught on, Oliver leaned toward me and said,

"Come on now, Kevin. You don't *really* think there's a separation of church and state in this country, do you?"

The price these people are paying for our occupation of their land is sadly self-evident. For it can be said with certainty that whatever benefits they are gaining by the operation of the boarding schools will be at the expense of the health of all and the lives of many of these children.

> - Indian Agent Gerald Barry, referring to the United Church's Ahousaht Indian residential school, October 18, 1940

I've lost my job but not my calling.

> - Kevin Annett, quoted in "Minister who tried to bring natives into the fold fired by his church" by Stephen Hume, Vancouver Sun, July 10, 1995

Canada and its churches, along with their sponsors in London and Rome, committed a deliberate and massive campaign of genocide against aboriginal children for over a century. Under the Law of Nations such a criminal regime has lost its right to govern or expect allegiance from its citizens, and the people are morally and lawfully obligated to neither fund nor obey such a regime.

> - From the verdict of the International Common Law Court of Justice In the Matter of The People v. Ratzinger, Windsor et al, Brussels, February 25, 2013

Chapter Six: Opening the Floodgates – The Little Matter of Genocide

The Gang of Four may have successfully sealed their sordid land deal and lined their already-stuffed pockets, but in so doing they opened a bigger Pandora's Box whose lid was impossible to close. And that, of course, was Christian Canada's mass murder of brown children in that other deadly church-state contrivance misleadingly called the Indian residential schools.

Port Alberni was the flashpoint, the centre of the storm, since it had been the nexus of the European missionary invasion during the mid and latter 19th century. Its crimes were the most recent and the hardest to conceal, since their evidence was everywhere, and remembered by many still-living aboriginal eyewitnesses. And so the seemingly-defeated efforts of Earl George, Bruce Gunn and me soon triggered a new movement that even the Octopus could not contain.

It began in 1995, the year I was fired. Expelled and prevented from working in the United Church for not helping mask their company secrets, I had moved back to Vancouver with my wife Anne and our two daughters, who were still only three and six years old. Unaware that Anne was already meeting secretly with church officials who were funding her upcoming divorce action against me, I blithely enrolled that fall at the University of B.C. in a doctoral program in native studies.

As much as I wanted to retrain and move past the trauma of the past year, my heart was still among the Ahousahts, and all the other shut out and stepped on people who I had worked with. But most of all, I was determined to know why Earl George and I had faced such destruction after writing our letters to the government and the United Church. I sensed there was a deeper and more odious reason for our targeting, but it lingered somewhere, waiting in the wings.

It finally appeared, in the form of Harriett Nahanee and a sidewalk protest.

In mid-December of 1995, a handful of my friends had gathered with me outside the provincial United Church headquarters in Vancouver's upscale Kitsilano neighbourhood. Our protest placards read *"Where is justice in the United Church?" "Reinstate Reverend Annett"* and *"Come clean on your genocide!"*. The media was there in force, drawn by some sympathetic press coverage I'd received the previous summer, and by their brief hunger for a local David and Goliath story.

I didn't notice Harriett until she approached me. She was an aged aboriginal woman with stern grey eyes. I was handing out my press statement to reporters when she announced to me,

"I was in the Alberni residential school. I saw Principal Caldwell kill a little girl there."

The reporters flocked to her words. The next day, Harriett's story was splashed across a half page of the Vancouver Sun: *"Claim of murder goes back to '40's"* (see Figure 19). And so it began.

In *The Art of War*, Sun Tzu observed that a larger and more powerful adversary can be goaded into any action and prove to be an unintentional ally, provided that one first "forms the ground" of any battle. The United Church has certainly proved that adage time and again, commencing on that cold December day. For within two days of the *Sun* article's release, the United Church National Secretary, Virginia Coleman, issued a frantic press release to Canada's media denying any knowledge of the "alleged" murder, or of any involvement in a cover-up. But at that point, nobody had accused her church of a cover-up.

"I love it when they expose themselves like that" Bruce Gunn chuckled over the phone soon afterward, when he congratulated me on our action. "It was their guilty way of saying, 'Yes, we did do it.' "

The proof of the church's criminality emerged fast and furious after that. Two days after Harriett's account of the murder of the young girl – whose name was Maisie Shaw, age 14, from the Nininaht Indian nation – a second eyewitness, Archie Frank, came forward publicly to name the same Principal Alfred Caldwell as the killer of another child: ten year old Albert Gray, a young boy in Ahousaht. The account of Caldwell's murderous deeds once again emblazoned the pages of the Vancouver Sun: *"Beaten to death for theft of a prune"*. *(Figure 20)*

The United Church went into an immediate tailspin. One of the church officers who'd arranged my firing, Brian Thorpe, met with my wife Anne the day of the Albert Gray revelation and asked her to begin her divorce action against me. Four days later, on Christmas eve, Anne told me that she wanted a divorce. Soon after that, Thorpe, in the name of the church, began "delisting" procedures against me that would strip me of my license to practice as a minister.

But killing the messenger would not stop the tsunami we had unleashed. On February 1, 1996, barely a month later, the first class action lawsuit by Alberni residential school survivors against the United Church was launched in the B.C. Supreme Court. The fifteen plaintiffs, many of whom I knew or had been in my congregation, claimed they'd been sexually and physically tortured while under United Church incarceration. They demanded compensation and owning-up from both church and state. *(Figure 21)* But these assaults were the mere tip of an enormous and monstrous crime that spanned generations, and that our fledgling campaign began to surface over the subsequent years.

Mandatory sterilizations, routine floggings and starvation, slave labor, electrical tortures, the extensive trafficking of children and even babies: these and dozens of other atrocities all defined as genocide under international law were part of the daily menu at Indian residential schools. They all began to surface publicly from the account of our living eyewitnesses. *(The full evidence is in my book at www.murderbydecree.com)*

Nowadays, after years of official whitewashing, obfuscation and obstruction of justice by church and state, the horror of these revelations has been lost . But in 1996 their impact on the public and the media was profound.

For three years, until the federal government began its "Aboriginal Healing Fund" and other efforts to buy off and shut down the eyewitnesses and survivors, the Octopus was in a state of real confusion and defensiveness over the emerging fact of the genocide it had engineered. As a result, a few of us – Harriett Nahanee, me and a few dozen mostly native people – were able to "define the narrative" and force the country to face the fact of its Group Crime. The sparks that we had lit in Port Alberni over the Ahousaht land theft eventually kindled into a firestorm that swept the nation.

In response, the Octopus turned to its loyal junior partners, the state-funded band council native chiefs, to contain and divert the whole issue. On April 14, 1996, soon after the first class action residential school lawsuit against the United Church and the federal government had begun, a secret meeting was held in, of all places, my former church in Port Alberni. This confidential conclave was presided over by the United Church's two top officers, Moderator Marion Best and National Secretary Virginia Coleman, who had invited their counterpart- aficionados of the local Nuu-Chah-Nulth Tribal Council (NTC).

We know the details of what went on at this meeting because Bruce Gunn was present, like the proverbial fly on the wall, or snake in the grass, depending on your point of view.

With a foresight unusual for church bureaucrats, Marion and Virginia brought along their cheque book. Brandishing an offer that she was no doubt sure the chubby NTC chieftains would not refuse, Virginia announced,

"The United Church is willing to provide some monetary compensation to a limited number of former residential school students, but only on two conditions."

One can assume that at this point, visions of something more than sugar plums danced in the heads of the plump Indians present, all of whom had learned the score while children in the Alberni residential school. Virginia continued,

"The first condition is that you must agree to restrict all residential schools litigation to personal injury matters and not those of a criminal nature, like the alleged deaths of children. The second condition is that you must disassociate yourselves from Kevin Annett and all of his claims of murders in the Alberni residential school."

Our faithful observer, Bruce Gunn, said that he was surprised by the speed with which the aboriginal "leaders" gobbled up the deal. Nelson Keitlah, my erstwhile friend and supporter, was the first to jump and swallow what was offered, along with Cliff Atleo, Francis Frank and the more obviously crooked chiefs. But the deal was not struck until substantial personal benefits to the chiefs were agreed to by the United Church officers.

Not surprisingly, an atmosphere of good will and "reconciliation" prevailed among the pale and brown skinned mandarins who were present that night. That spirit of course did not extend to anyone outside the Arrangement: especially to me, my family, or any of the thousands of residential school "survivors" who could now expect, at best, a few drops of blood money and a legal gag order.

Those few Canadians who sometimes wonder why no native politician in Canada has ever called for a criminal prosecution of the churches that killed 60,000 of their own relatives should ponder the Port Alberni meeting of April 14, 1996. For that night's Arrangement set the pattern for all of the subsequent concealment of Genocide in Canada by the churches that did the killing and their willing mind-swabbed accomplices who call themselves "First Nations leaders".

Bruce Gunn grew profoundly discouraged after what he witnessed that day; or so he claimed, after the fact. He soon retired from the United Church to a private counselling practice in the far north of British Columbia after his own wife, too, filed for divorce. Or perhaps another deal had been worked out, for Bruce kept his distance from me after that. Fortunately, others stepped forward to take his place, for awhile. But at the end of the day, and after many unsuspected years, I learned that Fate and the survivors had chosen me to lead this burgeoning battle.

....

Nobody ever used the word "genocide" before Raphael Lemkin did, in 1944. The practice of exterminating entire groups operated for centuries before Lemkin came along. Genocide was the mainstay of the Imperium called Christendom that came to control Europe and most of the world. But there was no name for this greatest of crimes, any more than a lion has a lexicon for its gazelle-munching.

Our Christendom culture extinguished, both peacefully and violently, every Other it encountered as a reflex: habitually, continually, and with deep religious and moral conviction. But then and now our name for the deadly practice is different than what it actually is: like an Act of Faith, or the Civilizing of the Savages; and, in Canada, Christianizing and Assimilating, or today, Reconciliation.

Raphael Lemkin changed all that by trying to call black, black. His preferred term "Genocide" is from two Greek words meaning "killing a group". But even that term is inaccurate, as Lemkin himself pointed out in his five definitions of what the crime is: for only one part of any group had to be targeted for extermination in order for genocide to be going on. That's what the so-called Convention on the Crime of Genocide still says, which was adopted by the United Nations in 1948, but of course has rarely been acted upon.

As Polish Jews, fifty of Lemkin's family went up the chimney at Auschwitz and Treblinka during World War Two, so the guy knew what he was talking about. But ultimately his hopes for an enforceable law to curb the crime vanished in smoke, like his relatives had. Canada played a major role in yanking the teeth from the Genocide Convention and redefining the word itself, since like the British and the Americans, we knew very well that in theory our country would be the first one in the docket in a war crimes trial if the Convention remained as Lemkin had written it. Why? Because what we were doing to the Indians met all of Lemkin's criteria for genocide, which to him had three aspects: physical (killing people), biological (preventing births) and cultural (wiping out language and identity).

In the words of the future Canadian Prime Minister and liberal humanitarian icon Lester B. Pearson, who served as the External Affairs representative at the United Nations in 1947 during the debates on Lemkin's proposed Genocide Convention, "If the present draft *(of the Genocide Convention – KA)* is allowed to stand, I am afraid that our government will be unable to deny that its existing policies toward our Indians constitutes such a crime. For is not the forced education in a foreign tongue and the denial of daily contact with one's natural family, which occurs routinely in our Indian schools, an act of genocide, according to this draft? ... Since it is unfeasible to close these school facilities without risking a major breach with the churches who own and operate them, another means must be found to protect our government from the consequences of this draft. Surely that must involve a fundamental reconceptualizing of the word itself ..." (37)

Sure enough, after Lester Pearson and his ilk went to work, the very meaning of genocide was so reworked as to make it inapplicable to the atrocities being waged against aboriginals in the western world. This happened in two ways.

First, genocide was redefined not as an *act* (as Lemkin had done) but as *an intent to commit an act.* Secondly, the new definition stated that genocide was primarily physically violent in nature, rather than being (to quote Lemkin's original draft) "any commission or omission that seeks to undermine, extinguish or destroy the essential foundations of a culture over time."

Lemkin had stated plainly "Genocide means the destruction of a group, or part of a group". Such a broad meaning automatically condemned every government or major religion in the world. And so the *revised* Genocide Convention says this: "Genocide means *the intent to destroy*, in whole or in part, any national, racial, cultural or religious group." The intent, not the act?

Any lawyer can tell you the great difficulty of proving intent in a court of law. It's even more difficult when many people are involved in a crime, for how can there be such a thing as a single, shared intent among say an entire nation?

By calling the crime an intention rather than an action, the Genocide Convention's revisions created an enormous loophole through which any criminal corporation, government or church could escape, since discerning the intent behind their group crimes would be impossible without clear declarations of murderous purpose. In effect, this caveat prevented any nations or institutions from being tried for genocide: only individuals. And that of course was the purpose of the revisions.

All of this has great relevance to understanding how and why legal genocide and its subsequent cover-up and exoneration has happened so easily in Canada. Over the years, I discovered the reasons on the ground by combating the institutions responsible. But the proof is all around us, for it is the dank medium in which every Canadian swims.

Most of my countrymen and women refuse to believe me when I tell them that Indians on reservations in Canada are not citizens under the law but children, as "wards of the state"; or that a standing but unofficial "do not resuscitate" policy governs Indians who are admitted to hospitals in a life-threatened condition; or that unlike any other ethnic group, aboriginal children can be seized from their parents by social workers or police without a court order or any kind of review process; or that the federal government subsidizes penitentiary officials twice the amount for an incarcerated Indian than they do for any other prisoner.

What this all points to is the continued "two standards" policy governing any group targeted for long-term eradication: a double standard when it comes to legal rights, health standards or due process. How is it, for instance, that Canadian policemen – especially Mounties – routinely shoot Indians to death without provocation and are never even reprimanded?

These kind of institutionalized killings against a targeted group like Indians happen for the simple reason that there will be no legal consequence for the killings. Aboriginal people in Canada are in practice subordinated non-citizens, as "Nullus" as they were at the time of first contact; and as expendable.

Knowing this, it is understandable why not a single person, let alone a responsible official of church and state, has ever been charged or tried in Canada for the death of the more than 60,000 children who died in the Indian residential schools internment camps. For that genocide was not only legally sanctioned but morally condoned by every level of society.

Quite simply, it was not a crime then, and it isn't one now.

Of course, Canada is not unique in this regard, for any genocidal regime must operate according to such Two Standards of legality and morality in order to maintain its control over the lands and wealth it has stolen from the targeted populace. This is especially true in a country as vast and resource-rich as Canada, whose economy rises and falls according to the external demand for those resources in foreign markets. And how very indicative of this fact was the speed and efficiency with which Earl George and I faced the unrelenting wrath and assault by the United Church when we brought to light the tag-team theft of Ahousaht land by itself and its government and corporate partners.

Ironically, despite its vaunted power to smash and silence, the Canadian Octopus is terribly vulnerable. For as the historic offspring of Empire and of Imperial dependency, it has always been the child and pawn of foreign interests: first British, then American, and now Chinese.

Like the pathetic slave-chiefs on the state-funded Indian band councils, the pale heads of Canadian churches, companies and governments are at best branch plant managers; and as such they have a deep fear and uncertainty about their tenuous hold on their own power. That explains in part their fierce, knee-jerk and unstrategic treatment of their critics, as was demonstrated by the very hurried and panicked United Church press release denying that they covered up Maisie Shaw's death. The small case illustrates the nature of the whole.

And so while the revelation of the Canadian Holocaust seems to have disturbed the sleep of very few "mainstream" Canadians and has not slowed the extermination process by one bit, and even as the churches responsible for destroying generations of Indian children carry on unpunished and self-exculpating in their secure little world, guarded by the law, the little matter of our home-grown genocide stands revealed. But what lies exposed is not some dry historical record or a carefully-hewn and meaningless "apology" for slaughter, but a continuing, ravaging beast that consumes the land and degrades the national soul of we, the Muu-Multh-Nees: the Ghost People.

The Ahousahts did indeed foresee the future when our lost

ancestor-wanderers arrived on their land. For as Nelson Keitlah related to me, the female Christ who came among them to warn of the coming pale invaders declared, *"You are to wait for the whites to destroy themselves, and then reclaim your land and your lives"*.

And so, at the end of the day, a remnant does survive even the worst atrocity: but only from within the ranks of the still-living. Meanwhile, the Dead continue to hold official sway: both the rulers and their puppets.

"Hey, didn't I see you on the Lone Ranger?"
AFN "Grand Chief" Shawn Atleo does his Indianness routine for Prime Minister Stephen Harper, who isn't fooled by the hat

The Directors and the Ha-wiih are pleased to report a record year in earnings. With market development, Lisaak will continue to pursue markets that provide the highest return. Lisaak is developing a highly unique and readily recognizable marketing strategy aimed at local and specialty markets for wood products as well as a range of other forest products that can benefit from the "Clayoquot" brand name.

> *- Ahousaht Band Council's Lissak Forest Resources Company's Annual Report for 2016, describing the logging of the Clayoquot Sound old growth forests*

We're the power now and that means making ourselves sustainable, that's the word you keep hearing from the board room people, the need for sustainable development. There's no loans if we aren't sustainable and that means getting rid of the dead wood on the reserves and in our territories, and making our Nations economically viable, team players at the international level. We've got to become the new G7, I want that. But we've got to face the facts, we've got to do what all the other Nations did to get productive. Sure there's a human cost in that, but that's the price you pay for progress.

> *- Wendy Grant-John, sub-chief, Musqueam Indian Band, speaking to a closed session of the Chiefs in Council at the Regional Conference of the Assembly of First Nations, Calgary, June 2, 2008*

Yes, it's accurate to say that half of the children died in those places. But if we allowed the full story to come out and let all those people speak, the churches would end up going bankrupt and I don't want that. The past is probably best forgotten.
- Murray Sinclair, "Aboriginal" Chairman of the Truth and Reconciliation Commission hearings into the Indian Residential Schools, Winnipeg, October 9, 2013

In the man of color, there is a constant effort to run away from his own individuality, to annihilate his own presence.
- Frantz Fanon, **Dark Man, White Masks**

Chapter Seven: Aftermath – What is this Thing called Neo-Colonialism?

Like most pale Canadians who bother to notice them, I had a romantic view of Indians for most of my life.

I remember how at the age of five I was distinctly disappointed and utterly disbelieving when I encountered some aboriginals at the Calgary Stampede, since they didn't dress or act any different from the rest of us down-home boys in our cowboy hats and boots. The real red skins had to be hiding out somewhere, I figured. So later that day I went searching for them, and I threw a scare into my parents when I vanished into the crowds. Eventually they found me, my top half stuck inside the canvas of one of those Made For Tourist Tee-Pees.

"What the hell were you doing in there, Kev?" my father asked me, half-amused, after he'd yanked me out.

"I was looking for some real Indians" I declared.

Ironically, I spent much of the subsequent half century of my life doing precisely that, without much luck.

Conquering powers always create imaginary images of the people they're destroying. They need to do so initially in order to kill most of the Others, and subsequently to tame and train the survivors as their servants. The greater the level of extinction, the more fanciful becomes the dominators' view of the exterminated ones. Hobbes, Voltaire, Rousseau and other European intellectuals demonstrated this in spades in their fanciful depictions of the "noble savage" in a pristine state of nature.

Closer to home, the very same Canadian civil servant who oversaw the early, massive killing-off phase of the Indian residential schools – Duncan Campbell Scott, the Superintendent of Indian Affairs – was an accomplished man of letters and celebrated author who wrote long poems extolling the virtues of the very Indians he was destroying. (38)

A continuing echo of this self-serving myopia about our victims can be heard in the present day prattle of Canadian politicians, media pundits and academicians about the so-called and imagined "healing and reconciliation" between whites and Indians; or I should say, the *right kind* of Indians.

The "right" kind, for those of you who don't know, are the Indians who never use the word genocide or speak of mass graves of children. They're the ones who smile for the cameras, forgive and forget everything, and thankfully accept a few dollars of blood money to "compensate" them for their destruction.

Unfortunately, these domesticated Indians – the "Uncle Tomahawks", or Around the Fort Indians, as they're called among actual native people – are the only ones who mainstream Canadians are allowed to see on the evening news, since they have been manufactured and groomed to perform that house-trained role for the cameras.

In reality, the collaborating, state-funded "chiefs" are the aboriginal creation of the same genocidal system that wiped out 90% of their families and friends. These assimilated "leaders" not only live, think and look like their white masters: they are them. And that, of course, is part of the perverted genius of Genocide's equally-evil twin known as Neo-Colonialism.

While he lived, nobody understood this tragedy better than Earl Maquinna George.

As Earl struggled alone to preserve a shred of his ancestors' spirit and his duty under their law to preserve the land and oppose the clear-cut logging, Earl's biggest opponents were his own people and his colleagues on the Ahousaht band council. Earl became as estranged from the mainstream vested interests of his own culture as I eventually did from mine, and for the same basic reason: he refused to put his own integrity second to big money. Earl George wouldn't be part of the inside corporate arrangement between the other chiefs and Weyerhauser to chop up and profit from the last remaining cedar forests of the Clayoquot Sound.

One of Earl's biggest adversaries, the Atleo family, is at the heart of this farce. "Chief" Cliff Atleo greased the wheels that landed Lot 363 in the hands of first MacMillan-Blodedel and then Weyerhauser. Cliff then cooked up the joint venture company with Weyerhauser known as Lisaak Ltd., which as you read this is the only logging company killing off the remnant Clayoquot rain forests. And to top it off, Cliff's own son Shawn Atleo went on to head the collaborating "Assembly of First Nations" (AFN) and launch similar "red washing" deals between resource multinationals and native bands across Canada.

From the viewpoint of the Atleos and their kind, there's no other game in town to play. Of course, even if there was one they would never dare to play it; for that kind of independence and courage was bred and battered out of them long ago in residential school. This trauma-based conditioning and mind control was after all a central purpose of those schools.

In a perverse sort of way, ab-original, state-crafted Indian chiefs have always reminded me of trade union bureaucrats; not only by the degree and pedigree of their domestication, but by their divided, two-faced role of loyal servant of the system and articulator of some of the rage and discontent of the people they claim to represent. This position requires that labor and Indian leaders make routine, safe protests about particular wrongs and threaten all kind of militant actions that never quite happen, simply to squeeze more out of the system to which they are loyally bound. But doing that as a profession fills a lot of them with a frustrated sense of inadequacy that they can only vent downwards, on their own people, and especially on dissidents who remind them of their lost and better selves, like Earl Maquinna George.

Slave psychology aside, the aboriginal comprador elites have been the primary means by which the pale genocide has increasingly wiped out the lingering remnants of indigenous culture and their occupation of the land. An honest examination of the archival record and the oral accounts of the vanishing, unassimilated survivors bears this out in graphic detail.

For example, it was the band council chiefs, put in place as early as 1876 by the Indian Act of Canada, who corralled their people onto reservations and their children into residential schools. They were the ones who enforced the outlawing of their own potlatching and round dancing ceremonies and their traditional medicines, and who arrested and jailed their own traditional leaders. (*See Figures 22 and 23*) As with the Nazi-collaborating Judenrat and Jewish Elders' Councils in Europe during the 1930's and '40's, the state-approved aboriginal puppet governments in Canada have been the ones who have done the on-the-ground exterminating for the dominant colonial powers.

If anything, that liquidation-job by the puppet chiefs has expanded in recent years as the value of indigenous resources has intensified along with the urgency to remove any impeding Indians from the path of the corporations hungry for them. Chinese, Japanese and other conglomerates normally pay the band council chiefs handsomely to act as "aboriginal consultants" or (as in the case of the west coast timber contracts) as joint-venture business partners. It was the national chiefs of the AFN who spoke out the strongest in favour of free-trade agreements not only between Canada and the USA but corporations and their own Indian bands.

Even more odiously and in the pay of the same corporations, the same chiefs have had a direct hand in evicting from their lands and killing their fellow Indians, trafficking native children and operating the growing drug trade among both urban and reservation Indians. It's a common complaint from many of my native contacts that the biggest suppliers of cocaine, crack and crystal meth on their reservations are the local chief or one of his relatives.

In addition, one of the unstated terms of so-called "treaty agreements" is that band council chiefs will expel a set quota of their fellow aboriginals from the rolls of certain key reservations on or near lucrative resources, especially in B.C. This requirement means routinely denying whole families, and many children and elders, access to housing, jobs, education and government subsidies, with the effect of driving them into poverty, homelessness, prostitution and suicide.

In effect, the band council chiefs have taken over the

murderous role originally performed by church missionaries and Indian agents.

"Our so-called chiefs are the problem today" said Carol Martin, a descendent of a matrilineal blood line of the Nisga'a Gitanyow Nation.

"They're implicated in our women going missing. I can name three top politicians with the First Nations Summit who are all convicted rapists, but naturally they're never charged. They've been trying for years to wipe out the traditional leaders of our tribes, the clan mothers, who always held original title to the land of their territories. That's what's really behind all the missing women, whether it's in Vancouver or Prince George." (39)

As a public critic of the collaborating chiefs, Carol Martin along with her four children have been routinely targeted by the government as well as the police in Vancouver. Since the Vancouver Olympics of 2010, Carol has been repeatedly arrested without being charged, and her children seized without notice by agents of the provincial Ministry of

Children and Families (MCF). The latter agency was in recent years run by Chief Ed John, a millionaire government-insider and aboriginal politician from Prince George who has been continually named as the head of a child and drug trafficking network operating among the Carrier-Sekani and other tribes in northern B.C.

Les Geurin is a member of the Musqueam Indian band in Vancouver. He knows first hand of Ed John's connection to crimes against his own people, and shared some of what he knew with me in the summer of 2004.

As the former maintenance man at the Musqueam Indian reserve where Ed John still resides as a band council chief, Les Guerin witnessed continual criminality by John and his employees between 1996 and 2004. These acts included illegal evictions, protection and strong-arm rackets, drug, weapons and child trafficking, and an apparent body-parts dumping operation by Dave Picton, the brother of convicted serial killer Willie Picton.

"Eddie John and his wife Wendy Grant-John run all the dirty

stuff on the reserve, like forcing families out of their homes and then seizing their property. Wendy's big into that. *(note: see her quote at the start of this chapter).* Or bringing in overseas drugs and guns at the Celtic Shipyards next to the reserve, them and their RCMP buddies. I even saw Dave Picton bring plastic bags onto the reserve one night and bury them in a pit near the garbage dump. I dug it up later and it was a pile of dirt and bones."

At that point, Les handed me a report from the Simon Fraser University forensics laboratory.

"You can see I had the bones examined and it turns out there were some human bones mixed with pig remains, including a young woman's skull and femur. I told the cops and the media but nobody would do a thing about it, I got threatened and told to shut up. Everybody's too scared of Eddie John and his mob and government connections." (40)

In many ways these corrupt aboriginal chiefs are the Canadian equivalent of any third world dictator. The latter runs his country as a police state in the pay of foreign multinational corporations who require cheap and easy access to natural resources and a cowed and impoverished workforce. Indians in Canada are in fact an internally colonized people, without nationhood or identity, ruled over by programmed and state-dependent puppet leaders. That structural feature of Canada has remained constant for centuries and will not change; for it is required by a ruling corporate elite whose wealth and status are dependent on foreign interests hungry for natural resources which are all located on traditional native territories.

I had the misfortune once to enter into the inner sanctum of the top aboriginal puppets of the state-funded Assembly of First Nations (AFN). It was in Vancouver during the spring of 2005, and I was there as part of an Aboriginal Youth Suicide Prevention Walk to Ottawa. The AFN chiefs wanted our brief presence for their own public relations purposes.

Frankly, I thought for a moment that I had stumbled into the wrong place. The meeting had the feel and set up of a glitzy corporate convention, complete with five hundred dollar suits, lavish multi-media staging, and sagging tables of free food, booze and tons of assorted give-aways. The AFN delegates were even more bovine and corpulent than your typical company man, for they were mostly the self-appointed or nepotistically elected band council chiefs from across Canada. Sprinkled among them were a few token elderly women who'd say the opening prayers or the politically correct words at the right moment, when the television cameras were on. But the entire atmosphere of the place felt wrong, decadent, and consummately bourgeois.

A friend of mine, Wilf Price of Haida ancestry, was an AFN delegate for a few years before he couldn't stand it any longer. As he described once on my *Hidden from History* radio program,

"We never did anything but sit there and listen to speeches and vote they way we were told to. Basically we were there to make contract deals with corporations and get the government's so-called treaty process to come off without a hitch or any opposition. As a reward we got anything we wanted, and I mean anything. Free booze, free drugs, free women, or even a kid if you wanted one. I actually got handed an unlimited expenses credit card by the regional AFN guy who just laughed like I was stupid when I asked him if he wanted me to save receipts.

"The government people were in the background watching us the whole time, but they didn't need to. None of us would ever threaten our own gravy train. I thought of all of the messed up and hungry people back on our reserve, the kids without proper schooling or family, and I knew if I was to ever look them in the face again I had to get out and stay out of the AFN." (41)

Any observer of this charade may notice that the primary item on the AFN's agenda is the treaty process, and the related issue of what the comprador chiefs call being "Partners in Development". In fact, the so-called treaties are the latest phase in the genocidal extinction of Indians, mediated by the chiefs in exchange for benefits to themselves as the brown "Partners" of predatory foreign capital.

The so-called treaty process in Canada is a misnomer that has nothing to due with the actual practice of treatying under international law. In return for government money (that goes mostly to the council chiefs and their families), the "treaties" extinguish an indigenous nation's original title to its own lands and resources. It also alienates and reduces that nation to the status of a legal corporation: a municipality under Canadian law with the power to sell off its properties and wealth. **Signing a treaty means to finally extinguish one's own nation; it does not constitute a mutually benefiting agreement between two equal nations.**

"Partners in Development" is the AFN's equally obfuscating term for the joint venture contracts signed between the native elites and resource corporations. It's Part B of self-extinguishment. For once the land that historically could not be sold becomes a mere commodity and the nation just another corporate actor, the chiefs can use their position to transform themselves into a new exploiting class, an aboriginal bourgeoisie who are an essential link in a resource-exploiting hierarchy.

In fact, this scheme is now so advanced that the genocide of native nations in Canada is now effectively completed. What remnant of non-collaborating, lumpen-proletarian Indians still exists is dying off rapidly and "naturally" from induced poverty and disease.

This practice is not unique to Canada but has been normative throughout the British Empire and the Catholic Church's domains. The whole purpose of the missionary program by both powers was to first identify, separate out and train potential native collaborators in order to supplant and destroy the traditional culture and its leaders. Converts to baptism would be spared extermination in exchange for their help in destroying the rest of their people. And so the AFN and its putrid brand of Canadian neo-colonialism is the logical and natural outcome of this centuries-old system of "salvaging and saving a few of the best savages", in the words of Catholic Bishop and the scourge of the Ahousahts, Auguste Brabant.

Understanding this system of selectively "rescuing" people from themselves for the long-term purposes of invading

Empire is essential to grasping how and why legal genocide continues in Canada today. It also explains the means by which an element of native people have been incorporated into the profit-driven, land-consuming genocide machine.

Denouement - A Post-Canadian Reflection

Like most countries, Canada is a huge repeat crime scene, except that it's bigger than most and so there are many more places to hide the bodies and the murder weapons. One of the less obvious places for such concealment is within the very attitudes and norms of Canadians themselves, and especially the idea that there really isn't much of a crime going on at all.

We've looked at how the wiping out of entire nations of Others is an accustomed practice in what we call western "Christian" civilization, and how that carnage is always aimed first and foremost at grabbing the Others' land. Canada's west coast is a classic example of this plague and the Octopus of church, state and corporation that runs it; and how the process called genocide destroys and refashions both the victims and the conquerors alike in order to better serve that homicidal system while pretending that it's something else.

No lie can live forever, said Martin Luther King.

Unfortunately, it can and does, if people have need of the lie. Earl Maquinna George and I bore personal witness to this cruel fact, as do all the unnamed and forgotten little casualties of Christian Empire scattered in graves all over the west coast and beyond. The United Church of Canada has suffered not one iota from the terror they inflicted on all of us and on the land. Nor have their ebulliently blithe clergy and parishioners paused for an instant in their pleasant little rituals to be shaken by horror and remorse, let alone depart from their perverse Sodom. The same bloody business carries on as usual, whether in the sanitized church pews or the corporate and government boardrooms.

Nevertheless, something else is going on outside all of the careful arrangements and spin doctoring; indeed, beyond any human tinkering whatsoever. Unseen and untouchable, it shapes final outcomes and brings to ruin all of the best laid plans of criminals in even the highest of places. The Greek writer Aeschylus described it this way: *And even in our sleep, pain which cannot forget falls drop by drop upon the heart, until in our despair, against our will, comes wisdom through the awful grace of God.*

Perhaps more to the point is an observation from Alice Miller, who spent her life helping traumatized people (and cultures) know their truth and speak it in order to break the cycle of violence in which they are hopelessly trapped:

The truth about our childhood is stored up in our body, and although we can repress it, we can never alter it. Our intellect can be deceived, our feelings manipulated, and conceptions confused, and our body tricked with medication. But someday our body will present its bill, for it is as incorruptible as a child, who, still whole in spirit, will accept no compromises or excuses, and it will not stop tormenting us until we stop evading the truth.

Today, Canada has been presented its bill at more than a material level. The force presenting it is not seeking reparations, for nothing can restore to the earth or its people what has been torn from them and desecrated. **The Bill of Damages is actually a Statement of Closure and Eviction**. The frightened church men and politicians who have bleated for "closure" of the inconvenient fact of their crimes against Indians have been granted their wish, but not on the terms or in the way they'd hoped. For it is they who are now closed for business, terminated by the law of historical dialectics and entropy that causes even the strongest system of oppression to break down under the very weight of its success.

The signs of this great finishing are everywhere, outside the vacuous bubble that poses as everyday Canadiana. In Alice Miller's parlance, Canadians can deceive their minds, manipulate their feelings and drug themselves with soothing opiates, but the child-like truth of what they have done and what they are stands above the bubble of illusion, refusing to go away until the big lie collapses. And then the signs of Canada's ending will be as obvious to all of its people as it is now to those of us whose scars and suffering have taught us the truth.

Some of the evidence of our national demise was made clear to me even as it destroyed my old life and gave birth to a new one: as the secret tale of land grab and Ahousaht-extermination by my church gave me a glimpse of the incestuous trinity of power that has made the Canadian Holocaust so successful. I entered this battle accidentally; Earl Maquinna George was born into it. But somehow fate brought us together long enough to tear open the first breach in the great concealment of that Holocaust. We begin a process of national exposure that will continue long after our tale has been forgotten.

But was it worth it for you? a friend of mine asked me recently when she learned that I was writing this, my thirteenth book on the Great Canadian Killing. The short answer, of course, is no. As much as the whole murderous game has an expiry date and is winding down, the cost of confronting its wrong has been too enormous to warrant any sense of ultimate victory.

Challenging the Lot 363 land theft stripped from us most of what mattered, at the time. My cherished family and vocation were blown apart by greedy men within and without the United Church; Earl George was denied his own calling and his health was so shattered that he died, according to his son, of a broken heart.

On the other side of the barricade, the criminals in this drama became filthy rich and stole away into the night, while the land and the Ahousahts continued to be ruined. One does not recover from betrayal on such a scale. And whatever legacy Earl and I have left by our sacrifice cannot be understood and will be only dimly appreciated by those who may benefit from it. At the end of the day, the simple knowledge that we could have done nothing else than what we did is our only unspoken comfort.

Recently I walked again in the cold dampness of the remaining old growth rain forest of the Clayoquot Sound. All around me its mossy and ancient fecundity spoke to my weary heart of that which remains alive and eternal, despite all the destruction; and of how neither chainsaws nor plague-bearing missionaries can abolish the land and its spirit, which alone endures.

Walking alone yet so accompanied, I recalled then with a contentment beyond words that long after all the villains have crumbled to nothing the land of the Ahousahts will remain. The chimera of power and property, of corporate machinations and religious conquest, will all return to the nothingness from which they were imagined. And perhaps that is the meaning of the endurance of our witness: that all illusion must in the end surrender to truth, and be released. But only after the matter is forced.

The sickness of a nation does not kill Man. And yet should we continue to look upwards? Our ideal is terrifying to behold, lost as it is in the depths, small, isolated, a pin-point, brilliant but threatened on all sides by the dark forces that surround it: nevertheless, no more in danger than a star in the jaws of the clouds.
    - Victor Hugo, *Les Miserables*

Footnotes

1. There is no clear scholarly consensus about the length of time that the Ahousahts have occupied their land. Estimates range from 5000 years (among mostly non-native academics) to over 10,000 years ago (according to the Nuu-Chah-Nulth Tribal Council). Because of the contending interests of corporations, government and the Ahousahts' own land claims, the issue is hotly politicized, which constrains objective scientific reporting.

2. See the original research on this atrocity in Tom Swanky's book **The True Story of Canada's War of Extermination on the Pacific** *(amazon.com)* as well as my own work **Murder by Decree: the Crime of Genocide in Canada** (2016), Appendix Ten, pp. 389, *(amazon.com and online at www.murderbydecree.com)*.

3. See this site: *https://www.ictinc.ca/blog/the-impact-of-smallpox-on-first-nations-on-the-west-coast* . The typically-low estimate by this group of the indigenous population levels reflects the mainstream Canadian position.

4. Wikipedia fails to mention the deliberate nature of smallpox dissemination among Indian nations, the role of itinerant missionaries in the infecting, or the coordination of this outbreak on the west coast with the decline of the economic importance of the fur and whaling industries after the 1860's.

5. These documents are from records in the Government of Canada's RG 10 microfilm series, DIA File R7733, in Koerner Library, University of British Columbia, and cited in my book **Murder by Decree: The Crime of Genocide in Canada,** on *amazon.com* and at *www.murderbydecree.com* .

6. See the account of Guillod's statement in The *Victoria Times-Colonist* article of March 21, 2014, "*Our History: Smallpox decimated Huu-ay-aht culture*" at *http://www.timescolonist.com/our-history-smallpox-decimated-huu-ay-aht-culture-1.916541* .

7. See "Aristotle and Natural Inequality" by Daniel Foss at *http://www.shlobin-foss.net/papers/unequal.html* .

8. For a general background on Roman property law see the online Encyclopedia Brittanica at *https://www.britannica.com/topic/Roman-law* . It is significant that all modern day government identities depict the bearer's name in the all-capital lettering of the Roman slave-status Capita Diminutio Maxima.

9. See **A Brief Account of the Devastation of the Indies** by Bartholomeo de Las Cases (Madrid, 1542) and **Murder by Decree**, ibid, pp. 34-35. As a cleric who accompanied the early Spanish invasions of Middle America, de Las Casas was a first hand observer of the Vatican's policy of "Conversion or Slaughter".

10. See "Luther's Doctrine of the Two Kingdoms" in the publication of the Evangelical Lutheran Church of America, at *http://www.elca.org/JLE/Articles/931* .

11. The Gradual Civilization Act was promulgated before the advent of the Canadian nation, in the Upper Canada Legislature in 1857. The complete Act is at *http://caid.ca/GraCivAct1857.pdf* .

12. The United Church of Canada Act was assented to in Parliament after its initiation by Order in Council, as with the Indian Act. The former is also discussed and reproduced in **Murder by Decree**, ibid.

13. See **Raphael Lemkin and the Struggle for the Genocide Convention** by John Cooper (Herald Press, 2008) and **Murder by Decree**, ibid.

14. Note the diminishing of indigenous populations during the first and third decades of the 20th century, during the highpoint of the residential school crimes.

15. Since at least 1960 and with the formal closing of the Indian residential schools during the 1970's, the Canadian government and the Roman Catholic, Anglican and United Church have periodically swept their archives clean of evidence related to the names and registries of Indian children in the schools, accident and punishment reports, and death records. In terms of the latter, as early as 1903 the federal government stopped issuing annual reports of mortality rates during and after the admission of Indian

children into residential schools. The records listed in this book and in **Murder by Decree: The Crime of Genocide in Canada** are taken from the only extant and available collection of microfilmed Indian residential school records in Canada, from the UBC Koerner Library in Vancouver.

16. For a general map of the location of Indian residential schools across Canada as of 1920, see pp. 394 of **Murder by Decree**, ibid. Nearly three quarters of the schools were located in the western provinces, where the only remaining "unassimilated" Indian nations were located.

17. This information was gleaned from conversations between the author and Rev. Bruce Gunn and Chief Earl Maquinna George, and private correspondence shared by them, some of which is reproduced herein.

18. This general statistic was derived from **Body Disposal at Auschwitz: The End of Holocaust Denial** by John C. Zimmerman (1999).

19. The routine practice by residential school staff of falsifying death records was referred to by Dr. Peter Bryce in a report to Indian Affairs head Duncan Campbell Scott in 1907. In these documents, government officials agree to discontinue reporting total deaths in residential schools; taken from **Murder by Decree**, ibid.

20. From the records of the International Tribunal of Crimes of Church and State (ITCCS) and of the author. See **Murder by Decree**, ibid.

21. Ibid.

22. From Anglican Church of Canada records held privately by Campbell Quatel and quoted with his permission.

23. From the final report of The Community Task Force on Missing Women, Vancouver, March 8, 2007, and from the private records of the author.

24. From a letter from Alexander Sutherland to the Superintendent General of Indian Affairs, Ottawa, March 1, 1888.

25. From the Report of the Community Task Force into Missing Women, March 8, 2007, ibid.

26. As quoted in Kennedy, Mervyn Ewart, **The History of Presbyterianism in British Columbia, 1861-1935** (M.A. Thesis, UBC Department of History, 1938), p. 77.

27. This information was gleaned from conversations between the author and Rev. Bruce Gunn and Chief Earl Maquinna George and private correspondence shared by them, some of which is reproduced herein.

28. Quoted in Swanky, ibid.

29. From the Parliamentary Hansard, Ottawa, spring 1876.

30. See a discussion of this Papal doctrine in **Murder by Decree**, ibid., and in **The Inquisition of the Spanish Dependencies** by Henry Charles Lea (New York, 1908)

31. See **The Founding of Canada, Part Two** by Stanley Ryerson (Progress Books, 1960)

32. See Western Canada Wilderness Committee Educational report, Summer 1999, https://www.wildernesscommittee.org/sites/all/files/publications/1999%2005%20The%20fight%20to%20own%20BC%27s%20Forests.pdf.

33. See a detailed description of this sordid history in my books **Unrepentant: Disrobing the Emperor** (O Books, 2010) and **Unrelenting: Between Sodom and Zion** (Amazon, 2016).

34. From a statement by Win Stokes made on record at the United Church British Columbia Conference De-Listing Hearing that stripped me of my profession, September 5, 1996. From the notes of the author, Sheila Paterson and others.

35. As told by Earl Maquinna George to the author on January 13, 1994.

36. According to Bruce Gunn, to whom Anderson made the statement about the author at a church meeting in Kelowna, B.C. on June 5, 1995.

37. Cited in Cooper, ibid.

38. See *https://www.britannica.com/biography/Duncan-Campbell-Scott*

39. From an interview with Carol Martin on the author's radio program *Hidden from History* on February 5, 2007.

40. From an interview between Les Guerin and the author on July 9, 2004. See also **Murder by Decree,** ibid.

41. From an interview with Wilf Price on the author's *Hidden from History* radio program, July 2, 2008.

Index of Documents

Figure 1: Percentage of Christians among coastal Indians, 1902

Figure 2: Population Statistics, Aboriginals in Canada

Figures 3 and 4: Mortality rates in Indian residential schools, 1896

Figures 5 and 6: Government censorship of schools' mortality rates, 1903

Figure 7: Letter of Alexander Sutherland, Methodist Church, 1888

Figure 8: Comparison of Presbyterian and Catholic native converts, 1901

Figure 9: Letter of John Ross, 1914

Figure 10: Letter of Ahousaht Chief Billy August, 1914

Figure 11: Exoneration of John Ross for death of Carrie George, 1916

Figure 12: Land survey of Ohiat territory by Melvin Swartout, 1899

Figure 13: Letter of J.H. Edmison, Presbyterian Home Mission Board, 1917

Figure 14: Letter of Indian Agent Ashbridge, covering for United Church, 1940

Figure 15: Letter of Bruce Gunn, March 9, 1999

Figure 16: Letter of Kevin Annett re: Lot 363 sale, 1994

Figure 17: Petition-Appeal of Bruce Gunn and Kevin Annett, 1997

Figure 18: *Vancouver Sun* article re: Weyerhauser deal, 1999

Figure 19: *Vancouver Sun* article re: Maisie Shaw murder, 1995

Figure 20: *Vancouver Sun* article re: Albert Gray murder, 1995

Figure 21: *Vancouver Sun* article re: first residential school lawsuit, 1996

Figures 22 and 23: Collaboration of native chiefs in banning native art and incarcerating children in residential schools, 1905, 1940

Department of Indian Affairs:-
OTTAWA, 18th December, 1902.

erintendent General:-

Memo. re application of Rev. Dr Mackay, Secretary of the Foreign Mission Committee of the Presbyterian Church in Canada, for a grant towards a boarding school building at Ahousaht, B.C. and the maintenance of 50 children.

1. The census returns for the year ended 30th June, 1902, give the population of the West Coast Agency as 2,414, made up as follows:-

```
Presbyterians.......287
Methodists.........150
Roman Catholics.....631
Pagans.............1346
                   ────
                   2414
```

The total school population of this Agency is 415.

The Ahousaht Band numbers 273, two of whom are Roman Catholics, the remainder, 271 being given as Pagans. In the Census Returns for 1901, however, this Band was shown to have 277 members:-

```
Presbyterians.......100
Roman Catholics......69
Pagans..............108
                    ───
                    277
```

No explanation is given by the Agent as to why he counted them all as Pagans.

The number of children of school age in this Band enrolled at the day schoo   average attend-

Population and Migration

Series A125-163. Origins of the population, census dates, 1871 to 1971 (concluded)

Series no.	Origin¹	1871	1881	1901	1911	1921	1931	1941	1951	1961
154	Asiatic	4	4,383	23,731	43,213	65,914	84,548	74,064	72,827	121,753
155	Chinese	—	4,383	17,312	27,831	39,587	46,519	34,627	32,528	58,197
156	Japanese	—	—	4,738	9,067	15,868	23,342	23,149	21,663	29,157
157	Other	4	—	1,681	6,315	10,459	14,687	16,288	18,636	34,399
158	Other origins	52,442	173,527	127,092	157,317	157,996	157,925	189,723	354,026	
159	Native Indian and Inuit (Eskimo)	23,037	108,547	127,941 → 105,611	16,994	117,724	128,890 → 125,521	165,607		
160	Negro	21,496	21,394	17,437	18,310	18,648	19,456	22,174	18,020	
161	Other	348	2,780	145	627	661	36,753	170,40		
162	Not stated	7,561	40,806	31,539	15,932	211,949	8,898	5,275		
163	Total	3,485,761	4,324,810	6,371,315	7,206,643	8,787,949	10,376,786	11,506,655	14,009,429

¹ The data for 1871 refer only to the four original provinces of Canada. The data for 1961 and later years include Newfoundland.
² Includes Bohemian, Bukovinian and Slavic.
³ Included under Scandinavian.
⁴ Includes Lithuanian and Moravian.
⁵ Includes Bulgarian.
⁶ Includes Flemish and Polish.
⁷ Since 1921 Scandinavian has been divided into Norwegian and Swedish.
⁸ Includes Bukovinian, Galacian and Ruthenian.
⁹ Includes 35,416 Métis.
¹⁰ Origin "not stated" cases in 1971 were computer assigned.

Figure 2

Series A164-184. Principal religious denominations of the population, census dates, 1871 to 1971

Year	Anglican	Baptist	Congregationalist	Evangelical Church	Greek Orthodox¹	Jehovah's Witnesses	Jewish	Lutheran	Mennonite²	Methodist
	164	165	166	167	168	169	170	171	172	173
1971	2,543,180	667,245	—³	—⁴	316,605	174,805	276,025	715,740	181,800	—
1961	2,409,068	593,553	—³	27,079	239,766	68,018	254,368	662,744	152,452	—
1951	2,060,720	519,585	—⁴	50,900	172,271	34,596	204,836	444,923	125,938	—
1941	1,754,368	484,465	—⁴	37,064	139,845	7,007	168,585	401,836	111,554	—

> Cote, Assa.
> 26th Feb 1896.
>
> Report as to the status of children sent to Industrial Schools and who are not there now. See Circular letter No 9236, of 6th Feb, 96

Name.	Married, or single.	Remarks.
		Industrial School, Qu'Appelle.
No 1 Alfred Stevenson.	Married.	Supports himself. Works for Settlers, etc.
Catherine Que-ow-sance.	Single.	At service, Crowstand School.
Rod'k McLeod.	Single.	Dying. Consumption.
John McLeod.	Married.	Not strong, useless and lazy; not the fault of the school but himself.
Margaret McLeod.	Single.	Living with her Aunt, Mrs Anders Qu'Appelle.
Marie Que-ow-sance.	Single.	Died.
Angelique Cote.	Single.	Died.
Louis Cote.	Single.	Died.
Marie Josephine Bourassa.	Single.	Died.
Marie Louisa Bourassa.	Single.	Died.
Henry E-qua-nin.	Single.	Died.

Out of a total No of 13 sent to this school, 8 have died...

Over 60% of the Indian children at the Catholic Qu'Appelle school are dead or dying in the first year the school was opened – ie: seven of the eleven children listed (1896)

Figure 3

138550

Report as to the status of school children sent to Industrial Schools, and who are not there now.
See Circular No 0126 of 6th Feb 1896.

Name.	Married or Single.	Remarks.
		Industrial School, Regina.
Sam'l Ka-ke-we-ass.	Single.	Died.
Maggie Baldhead.	Single.	Died.
Jane Fiddler.	Single.	Died.
Jim Crow.	Single.	Died.
— Crow.	Single.	Died.
Lizzie Severight.	Single.	Died.
Maggie Torrengo.	Single.	Sent home, is dying of consumption.
Joe Cote.	Single.	Sent home, weak lungs.
Maud Cote.	Single	Sent home, weak lungs.
Alex Shinguish.	Single.	Blind, is recovering.
John Severight.	Single.	Recovering from effects of fever
John Cook.	Single.	Died.
		Industrial School, Elkhorn.
Shannon Coo-pa-pay.	Single.	Died at school.

sgd W.E. Jones.
Indian Agent.

Indian Affairs. (RG 10, Volume 3861, File 82,390)
PUBLIC ARCHIVES

Two thirds of the students are dead or dying (8 of 12) at the Catholic Regina Indian school in the second year of its operation (1896)

Figure 4

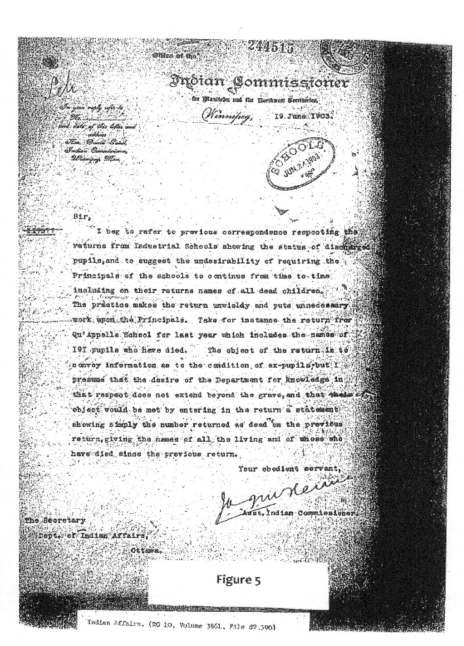

Figure 5

Indian Affairs. (RG 10, Volume 3861, File 82,390)

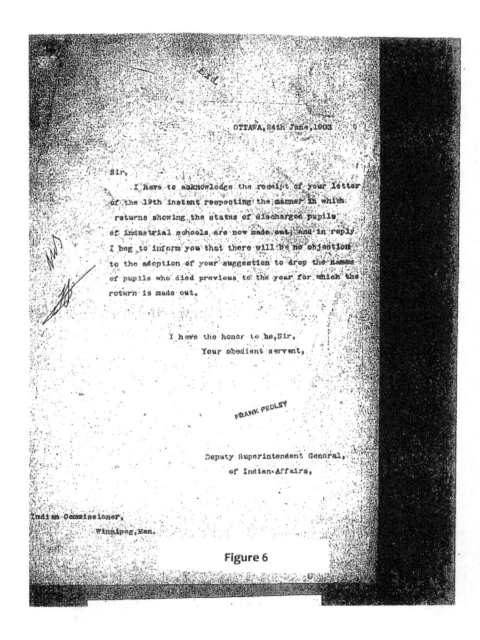

OTTAWA, 24th June, 1903

Sir,

I have to acknowledge the receipt of your letter of the 19th instant respecting the manner in which returns showing the status of discharged pupils of industrial schools are now made out, and in reply I beg to inform you that there will be no objection to the adoption of your suggestion to drop the names of pupils who died previous to the year for which the return is made out.

I have the honor to be, Sir,
Your obedient servant,

FRANK PEDLEY

Deputy Superintendent General,
of Indian Affairs,

Indian Commissioner,
Winnipeg, Man.

Figure 6

F. Zwan

Methodist Mission Rooms,
TORONTO, 1st March, 1888.

The Hon. the Superintendent General
of Indian Affairs,
Ottawa.

Dear Sir,-

As you have kindly intimated your willingness to meet Senator Macdonald and the undersigned to confer in regard to matters affecting Indian Schools, &c, I beg to submit for your information the following memorandum of points that we would like to have considered:

I. INDIAN SCHOOLS AND MISSION PREMISES IN ONTARIO.

On the 2nd April, 1883, I sent a communication in reply to two letters received from the Department in which I set forth our views in regard to the Industrial Institution at Muncey, and also in regard to our ordinary Indian schools. If the Superintendent General will kindly refer to that communication he will be in possession of the points we wish to present, so far as schools in Ontario are concerned.

In regard to sites for Mission premises on the different Reserves, we have frequently a good deal of trouble with the Indians, growing out of the fact that we have no legal or formal claim to any particular quantity of land. Sooner or later some grievance is sure to crop up, and some Indian will complain that we are occupying more ground than we are entitled to. We desire very much that this unsatisfactory condition of affairs should be ended, and we ask, therefore, that on all Reserves on which we have established missions there should be a distinct understanding reached between the Missionary Society, the resident Indian Agent and the Indian Department, in which the amount of land to be occupied for mission purpose should be clearly defined. Secondly, that the Department should give us a title of occupation (so long as we continue our mission work), protecting us alike from complaints of individual Indians, and also from trespass either by individuals or by the Band. This last request is owing to the fact that in some cases,- Cape Croker, for example;- the Indians have erected some of their own buildings upon land that was set apart for the use of the mission. Thirdly, if for any reason we should deem it expedient to withdraw from any particular Reserve, we desire either that the Department will take our buildings at a price to be fixed by arbitration, or else that we shall have a right to sell the buildings to any other purchaser who may offer to buy them.

II. SCHOOLS, &C, IN THE NORTHWEST TERRITORIES.

In regard to ordinary Indian Schools in the Northwest I beg to refer the Superintendent General to a communication of mine dated July 30th, 1883, in which the various points are presented in detail.

For the efficient carrying out of educational work among the Indians, we think it most important that provision should be made for Boarding Schools, and also for Industrial Institutions, where the children can be kept for a series of years away from the influences which surround them on the Reserves, and we call especial attention to the need ... ing locations.

Early church pressure   **Figure 7**   ls and thereby facilitate

1st, Lake Winnipeg. For more than forty years we have been carrying on educational and missionary work among the Bands around this lake, and to the north and east; but nothing has yet been done toward supplying either a boarding school or an industrial institution. We think that the work we have done among the Indians of that region entitles us to the consideration of the Government. 2ndly, Battle River. At the last session of Parliament the sum of $10,000 was voted for an Industrial Institution at Battle River, but so far as we are informed nothing futher has been done. The amount voted is entirely inadequate for an efficient institution, and is in suggestive contrast with the amounts expended on the institutions placed in charge of other religious bodies. 3rdly, the Morley Reserve. The Superintendent General is doubtless aware that an Orphanage and Training School have been established by the Missionary Society. Repeated applications have been made to the Government for buildings and a grant towards maintenance. Hitherto the first part of the request has been refused, while in regard to the second an annual grant of $700 has been made for the past two years, and recently a communication from the Department stated that Parliament would be asked during the present session to grant an amount equal to $60 for each pupil in the institution. There are very strong reasons why this institution should be enlarged in its scope, and made similar to those at Battleford, High River, Indian Head and Qu'Appelle, and the reasons which have led the Government to give such liberal support to these latter institutions apply with equal if not greater force in the case of Morley.

In regard to sites for mission premises our request is that in all cases they be excluded from the Reserves, so that we may obtain an absolute title to the property.

III. SCHOOLS IN BRITISH COLUMBIA.

What has been said about schools in the Northwest territories will apply, to some extent at least, to schools in British Columbia; but in regard to Industrial or Boarding Schools I would say that we regard an institution of the kind, located in the neighborhood of Chilliwhack in the valley of the Fraser, an urgent necessity. It has been rumored that the Government have in contemplation the establishment of two institutions, one on Vancouver Island and the other on the mainland, but that the latter is not to be located in the valley of the Fraser. I sincerely hope that this will not be the final decision of the Department, and that in the establishment and management of these schools, the work which has been done among the Indians by our Missionary Society will receive practical recognition. In this connection we beg to call attention to the needs of the Indians in the northern part of the province, where nothing has been done by the Government in the way of education, except in certain small grants made to particular mission schools. It is of great importance that some more advanced work be done in that region, especially on the line of industrial pursuits. In this connection I beg to mention the case of the Indian Girls' Home at Port Simpson, which has hitherto been supported exclusively by the voluntary gifts of Christian people. I think this institution is fairly entitled to consideration by the Government, and I hope that when the nature of the enterprise is understood, a grant will be made towards its maintenance.

Any further information I can give touching any of the foregoing points will be cheerfully furnished in a personal interview.

civilization they are working out for themselves
through necessity.

2. Although the Presbyterians are in a small majority at Ahousaht the census returns show that all the Indians on the surrounding reserves and to the north are either Roman Catholics or pagans. The Roman Catholic boarding school at Clayoquot draws its pupils chiefly from the section of country in which the Presbyterians wish to locate their boarding school, while the Methodists claim nearly all the Indians about Nitinaht (south-east of Barclay Sound) and would certainly object to any recruiting being done in their mission field. The last census credits the Presbyterians with only 375 adherents out of a total population of 2480 in this Agency, while the Roman Catholics have 961 and the Methodists 178 and the remaining 966 are given as pagans, who offer a field for missionary work for any religious body desiring to enter it, but they should do so at their own expense as the Department should not be expected to pay for making converts to any particular creed.

I do not see, therefore, that the Presbyterians have any strong claim to Government support for another boarding school at Ahousaht or elsewhere in the West Coast Agency at present.

3. I Figure 8 h instant I
referred to t   has to contend

COPY

Ahousaht, B. C., Dec. 24, 1914.

Dear Dr. Grant,-

I received your letter of December 11th with enclosure of a letter you received from the Indian Department, Ottawa. On Dec. 22nd, I had an interview with the young man, Alex Sutherland, who wrote the letter for the Indians of Ahousaht. Before Mrs. Ross, Miss McIvor and myself he confessed that the charges laid against me in the letter are false.

Although there is still some ill-feeling against me on the part of graduates of the Roman Catholic school and possibly a half a dozen of our own following, still almost all the Ahousahts are on friendly terms with us. Of course there has been trouble between myself and the Ahousaht Indians, but to be fair the Indians are not to be blamed so much when you know the whole truth.

For some time I have taken an active part in the suppression of intertribal potlatching. I was the first on the West Coast to lay information before the authorities of a breach of the Indian Act in regard to the custom. In spite of warning from the Indian Agent Cox and myself the Ahousaht Tribe gave   aht Tribe Nov,
-20th. As it was th   ans paid the

Figure 9

192

= 2 =

$10.00 to $15.00 on sea biscuits or rice to feed the entire tribe, which after all is no more than the average cost of Christmas in the majority of white homes in Canada. But the intertribal potlatching custom is bad. So long as it continues there is no possibility of Indian advancement in British Columbia. Of course, naturally, the Indian feels pretty sore about the new law and they were angry because I was the first to take up a case of the kind on the West Coast.

Now I wish to put the blame just where it belongs. The very day I was called away to give evidence on this particular case held in Clayoquot court, a Jesuit Priest landed here from Clayoquot. The Indians gathered together and the priest spoke to them in a body sympathizing with them and promised to help them. He told them that there was a law against intertribal potlatching but that he would use his influence to help them so that they could potlatch the Kelsomahts. Further I have Indian witnesses to prove that the letter written by Alex Sutherland to the Department was written in the presence of Father Joseph Schindler. Father Joseph did not write it with his own hand but he heard it discussed and was there while a rough draft of the letter was made. Only twice during 1913 was mass said in the Roman Catholic Chapel at Ahousaht, but every time a jesuit priest pays a visit to Ahousaht trouble is made for us. The following Sunday after Father Joseph had his meeting with the Indians he landed to say mass for one

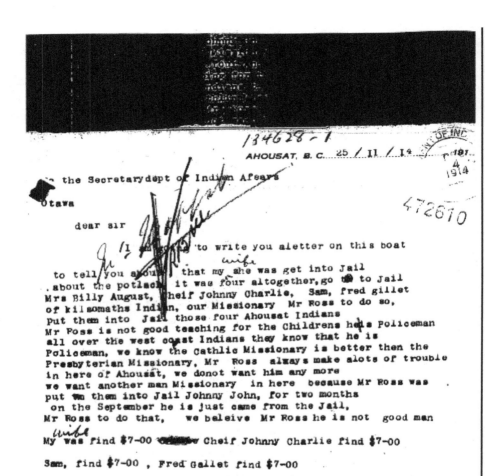

AHOUSAT, B.C. 25 / 11 / 14

the Secretary dept of Indian Afears

Otawa

dear sir

(I am going) to write you a letter on this boat
to tell you about that my wife she was get into Jail
about the potlach it was four altogether, go to to Jail
Mrs Billy August, Cheif Johnny Charlie, Sam, fred gillet
of kilsomaths Indian, our Missionary Mr Ross to do so,
Put them into Jail those four Ahousat Indians
Mr Ross is not good teaching for the Childrens he is Policeman
all over the west coast Indians they know that he is
Policeman, we know the Cathlic Missionary is better then the
Presbyterian Missionary, Mr Ross always make alots of trouble
in here of Ahousat, we donot want him any more
we want another man Missionary in here because Mr Ross was
put em them into Jail Johnny John, for two months
on the September he is just came from the Jail,
Mr Ross to do that, we beleive Mr Ross he is not good man

My wife was find $7-00 Cheif Johnny Charlie find $7-00

Sam, find $7-00 , Fred Gallet find $7-00

they pay to the Caurt,

yours truly

Billy August

Figure 10

134628-1

DEPARTMENT OF INDIAN AFFAIRS APR 13 1916

WEST COAST INDIAN AGENCY,

Alberni, B. C. April 6th, 1916.

Letter No.

489365

SIR,

I regret to enclose the resignation of the Rev. J. T. Ross of Ahousaht, together with his report of the unfortunate accident which caused the death of Carrie George, No. 062, pupil at the Ahousaht School.

Personally I am satisfied that Mr. Ross was in no wise to blame, as the child had evidently procured the matches from her home, as they were of a totally different manufacture to those used in the School.

Yours obediently,

Indian Agent.

The Secretary,

Dept. of Indian Affairs,

Ottawa.

Figure 11

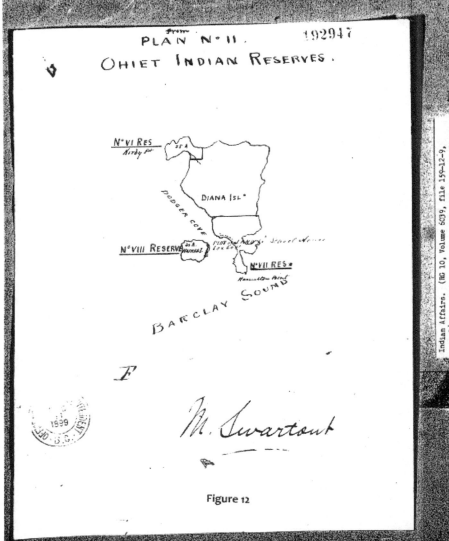

Figure 12

The Presbyterian Church in Canada
The Board of Home Missions and Social Service

434 CONFEDERATION LIFE BUILDING

Toronto, July 2nd, 1917.

D. C. Scott, Esq.,
Deputy Superintendent General,
Department of Indian Affairs,
Ottawa, Ont.

502086

Dear Mr. Scott:-

Following our interview with you June 15th, our Committee had a conference with representatives of the Women's Missionary Society, at which we drew up the enclosed recommendations.

These have been considered by the W.M.S Board and by the Executive of the Board of Home Missions and Social Service, and have been adopted by both Boards.

You will note that we propose to sell to the Government the land on which the other buildings are located. We suggest ten acres. This, of course, is the best part of the property. Mr. Currie values this land at $200 per acre.

The buildings unburned - that is; school, woodshed, barn, chicken house, etc.- we value at $3,000. Mr. Currie says they cannot be put up for this figure.

We do not propose that the Government shall pay cash for either the land or the buildings, but that the $4,000 shall become part of the advance to the Government.

Our W.M.S. have agreed to erect a house near the church at Ahousaht for the use of the missionary and his family, and the Field Matron, whom we expect the Government to appoint.

Our Board proposes sending a good missionary to Ucluelet to care for the whole district. We are planning to secure a launch for him.

In looking over these recommendations, I am sure you will be convinced that we are anxious to do everything in our power to assist the Government in caring for the Indian children. This $20,000 is all the money that is available at the present time.

Trusting the recommendations may find the approval of the Department,

Believe me,

Yours sincerely,

JH Edmison
Secretary.

Figure 13

Feb. 3, 1940.

Jan. 26, 1940. 6:30 pm
- school burned down

- 4 -

Agent's Report on fire at Ahousaht Residential School. (cont.)

School Nurse. The school nurse, Mrs. M.B. Griffin, is remaining, pending instructions, and I would recommend that she be retained at Ahousaht until the end of March, as she is doing valuable work in the village and can be of great assistance with the day school, if such is approved.

Remarks. As this school was the property of, and conducted by, the Church, care was taken to avoid too close inquiry.

Too much credence was not placed upon comments and theories advanced by different people, as all were more or less laboring under excitement and strain.

It is however my opinion that faulty wiring was the cause. It will be noted from my reports on this school that, due to its condition, I have at all times stressed the importance of fire drills and the upkeep of escapes.
Thanks to the discipline of the children, no one was lost or hurt.
Great credit is due to Mrs. Preece, Kitchen Matron, Mrs. Griffin, Nurse, and Mrs. Sainsbury, Sewing Matron, whom I am informed were instrumental in giving the alarm, evacuating the school, and mustering the pupils in a place of safety.

In conclusion I would respectfully request that authority be granted to expend up to the amount of $200.00, for the purpose of supplying clothing, bedding, etc. at discretion, in cases where hardship is being experienced due to influx of children in homes unprepared for them, and where parents are not in a position to supply necessities.

Respectfully submitted,

Your obedient servant,

P. B. Ashbridge,
Indian Agent.

PBA/AM

Figure 14

Indian Agent P. Ashbridge covers for the United Church during his "investigation" of deaths of children following a fire at the Ahousaht residential school (1940)

Statement of (Rev.) Bruce Gunn of Telegraph Creek, B.C.,
made to Kevin Annett in a phone conversation, March, 1999

The whole process of your firing was farcical. The church knew there were 1,400 lawsuits coming down the pipe over the residential schools. I'm convinced that your removal was orchestrated from Toronto, from the church head office. Just a week after you wrote your letter about the Ahousaht land deal, Marion Best (*UCC Moderator*) had a copy of that letter, since I gave it to Ria Whitehead, who chaired the World Mission annual meeting in Toronto that I attended, and Ria passed it directly to Marion Best. That would have been on the first weekend in November of 1994. Within a month of that, John Siebert of the head office was onto the case.

I think it's obvious, to me, that the national office removed you because they knew of the upcoming RCMP investigation, and of the land deal, after Marion Best got your letter. They were in for a rough fight and didn't want dissent from a Port Alberni pulpit.

There's no question that John Cashore (*UCC clergy and provincial Aboriginal Affairs minister*) tried to run interference for the church, and sidetrack the church connection to the land deal using government money, as early as the spring of 1994.

Cashore's role became pretty blatant long before your removal. At an August, 1994 meeting in Ahousaht set up to resolve the Lot 363 land deal issue, I objected to the government mediator, a Japanese fellow, that the United Church wasn't present, when they had owned and sold Lot 363. I asked him if their absence was related to the fact that the Aboriginal Affairs minister was also a United Church clergyman. <u>The mediator said that he wasn't aware about the church's role in it all, but that he was *"under instructions not to include the church"* in negotiations.</u>

At this same meeting, I said that I wanted to go on record as believing that John Cashore was in a conflict of interest over Lot 363, but it never got addressed, and Anne Atleo for the Ahousaht band council defended Cashore and denied he was in a conflict.

Some of the Ahousaht chiefs and myself met at St. Andrew's church in Port Alberni in September of 1994 to protest the church's absence from the talks. Cliff Atleo, Earl Maquinna George, Nelson Keitlah, Edwin Frank and two others wrote to Oliver Howard and Bill Howie of the United Church asking for the church to take some responsibility, but they never responded, nor did the communication ever appear in Presbytery minutes.

Figure 15

p. 2

At the same time, the band council was sidetracking Earl George because he wouldn't play along with Cashore and MacMillan-Bloedel over Lot 363. Earl's traditional role as Keeper of the Land put him in conflict with the band council's interest in negotiating a deal with MacMillan-Bloedel. So the council forced him out by not telling him of meetings and decisions. Louie Frank was the main instigator of this.

The payoff to the Ahousaht band council came from the United Church after a conference call with John Siebert and Brian Thorpe (*B.C. Conference Secretary*) that arranged to pay for research into the traditional oral claims of the Ahousahts regarding Lot 363. In the spring of 1995, $7000 went to the band council by way of the church's northern native group, run by Jim Angus. This $7000 went directly to the Ahousaht band council, and another $7000 bill for research was picked up by the church, making it a $14,000 payoff in all.

The church was at this same time cutting off Earl George's funding for ministerial training, and spreading rumours and smears against Earl among the Ahousahts. This whole thing was orchestrated mostly by Brian Thorpe with help from John Siebert.

I guess that's why John Cashore made sarcastic and disparaging remarks to Earl George about his ever becoming a United Church minister. It happened in April, 1994 in Ahousaht, at a ceremony, and Cashore said to Earl, with a smirk on his face, *"Do you think you'll ever become a United Church minister?"*. This was when Earl's candidacy was still before the courts of the church.

I raised an appeal on your behalf directly to the B.C. Conference president, Nina Cummings, at a division of World Missions meeting in April of 1995. But she never responded, anymore than she did about my appeals over Earl's candidacy.

It's also really significant, I believe, that George Ray Arthur, the man who bought much of Lot 363 from Hamilton Ross, after Ross got it from the United Church, was a big financial backer of the church. He donated money for the Christian Education Centre in Ahousaht all during the 1960's and '70's.

[signature]
Reverend Bruce W. M. Gunn

MINISTER: Rev. Kevin McNamee-Annett
Telephone: 723-8332.

The letter that got me fired
— Kevin

To the Officials and Members of
Comox-Nanaimo Presbytery
The United Church of Canada

St. Andrews United Church
Port Alberni, B.C.
4574 Elizabeth Street
Port Alberni B.C.
V9Y 6L6

Dear Members of Presbytery,   17 October 1994

    I am writing this in the wake of the brief discussion at the Fall Presbytery gathering in Gold River, concerning the issue of the Ahousats land settlement. I am both deeply concerned about the response of Presbyte officials to this issue, and the way in which this matter was dealt with a Presbytery.

    My perspective on this issue arises largely as a result of long and fruitful discussions with the Ahousats, including with several tribal elde The issue seems to be one of violated trust on our part, rather than any legalistic or documentary problem, as Presbytery officials have suggested. In a nutshell, native land was given to the Presbyterian, and then United Church, solely for the education and spiritual upkeep of the Ahousats, in particular the young people. This land was subsequently sold by the church to a private white individual. Simple justice and decency requires that ou church rectify our wrong by seeking the return of the said land to the Ahousats, and by publically admitting our mistake.

    This issue has been clouded over by our Presbytery. Some officials hav claimed that the Ahousats have created roadblocks to meeting, or cannot produce "appropriate" legal documentation to show ownership of the land by the Ahousats. Sadly, these are precisely the words and accusations that a colonial system has directed against indigenous peoples ever since we took away their land.

    The very fact that we are waiting for the Ahousats to prove their case to us, or to meet with us on our terms, reveals at best an insensitivity c the part of our church to God's call for justice towards those we have wronged; at worst, it indicates a perpetuation of the racist and oppressiv relationship that has been our legacy regarding indigenous peoples.

    It is not too late to reverse this legacy, or the wrong we committed : regards to the Ahousats land issue. Indeed, it is imperative that we do sc soon, if we are concerned at all about our credibility and integrity in tl eyes of both the indigenous peoples here, and the wider public.

    If we do not clearly and publically admit our wrong on this matter, ar seek actively to return the land in question to the Ahousats people, I wi find it difficult to associate myself with the United Church on this issu

    I urge Presbytery officials to meet immediately with the Ahousats eld on their terms, and come to a mutually-agreed resolution to this matter t upholds our paper position of supporting native land claims. Anything sho of this will expose a dangerous gap between our words and our actions.

Figure 16

Yours in Christ,
(Rev.) Kevin McNamee-An

Church, Government and Corporate Collusion in the On-going Take-over of First Nations Land: The Case of Lot #363 of the Ahousahts.

The sale and speculation of Ahousaht First Nation land on Flores Island (Lot #363) on Canada's west coast by the United Church of Canada, B. C. Provincial Government, MacMillan-Bloedel and two local businessmen was brought to light and challenged between 1992 and 1994. The two individuals primarily involved in making these disclosures, hereditary Ahousaht Chief Earl Maquinna George and United Church Minister The Rev. Kevin Annett, have now been expelled from the United Church over these same events. Their expulsions occurred simultaneously in the same two month period of December/January of 1994-1995, clearing the way for the subsequent consolidation of Lot #363 in the hands of MacMillan-Bloedel.

Lot # 363 consists of 100 Hectares of what is commonly regarded as among the most valuable stands of ancient rainforest Red Cedar on the West Coast of Vancouver Island. It is estimated to be worth in the millions of dollars. Against the wishes of local Ahousahts, who had provided the land for the Church to build a Residential school in 1904, the United Church sold Lot #363 in 1953 for $2,000. Chief Earl Maquinna George raised the unresolved issue of Lot #363 with Government and Church officials in correspondence as early as December 1992.(Exhibit #1) George asked that a way might be found for the Church to get the land back for his people.

In November/December of 1994, Officials of the United Church failed to provide funding necessary for the ministerial training of Chief George under a special Master of Divinity program of the Native Ministries Consortium. This prevented him from entering the ordained ministry of the United Church, even though Chief George's candidacy for ministry had already been approved by Comox-Nanaimo Presbytery and his academic requirements had been cleared by the Vancouver School of Theology. No written notification or explanation for this failure was provided. **During the ten year history of this joint Anglican -United Church funded program, Earl George was the first and only native chief in B. C. to present himself as a United Church candidate for this program.**

Within weeks of this action, and after having written a letter critical of the Church's handling of the Lot #363 issue (Exhibit #2), Kevin Annett's terms of pastoral ministry in Port Alberni were summarily changed, through the intervention of Church officials outside his congregation. Annett was removed immediately from his pulpit without stated cause, review, or advance notice. A letter was sent to him from the Church two days later advising him of the Church's intent to remove or "delist" him from ministry unless he complied with demands normally reserved for ministers under discipline. To this day the United Church has denied it has placed Kevin Annett under disciplinary action and /or the reasons for it. He is currently testifying before a precedent setting formal hearing in Vancouver as the last step of the church's delisting procedures.

Open letter by Kevin Annett and Bruce Gunn re: Ahousat land grab

Figure 17

At no point in the past two years has the matter of the Church's action against Rev. Annett been presented to the wider delegate bodies of the United Church, including his own congregation. The matter has been handled from its outset by a small Executive group whose actions are shared with wider church representatives through minutes "received for information" only.

Over that same two year period the land interests of the Ahousahts were further erroded with the purchase of an additional portion of Lot #363 by MacMillan- Bloedel in late 1994. The land is now being used in negotiation tactics to secure joint-venture access to the tree stands of Flores Island in the Clayoquot. This strategy has been aided and abetted by Aboriginal Affairs Minister, the Rev. John Cashore (a United Church Minister) whose actions have conveniently left the Church out of proposed negotiated settlements and contrary to the expressed wishes of the Ahousaht Chiefs.

It is our view that these extreme and unwarranted actions by the United Church constitute an attack on First Nations Peoples and those persons within the Church who uphold historic claims to Aboriginal lands. The United Church is attempting to silence Chief George and Rev. Annett to avoid public scrutiny of both its dealings with Lot #363 and the allegations of the murder of at least one native child by a senior church official at the United Church Residential School located on Lot #363 in 1938.(Exhibit #3)

The collusion of church, state and multi-national business officials in the take-over and exploitation of native land resources, specifically Lot#363, and the attempt to silence Chief George and Rev. Annett constitute a violation of both hereditary land claims and basic human rights. It also undermines the spirit and intent of the "new partnership" called for by the Royal Commission on Aboriginal Affairs. These actions by United Church officials are at complete variance with the history, conscience and soul of the United Church of Canada.

CALL FOR ACTION:

1. We call on the World Council of Churches to undertake an investigation into these actions of the United Church of Canada with respect to the treatment of Chief Earl George and the Rev. Kevin Annett, and to establish an International Tribunal to provide an appeal forum and process to ensure fair and impartial rulings on these human rights violations by its member churches. We also call on the World Council of Churches to assist in the establishment of a public forum in which Kevin Annett's suitability for ministry can be fairly and objectively evaluated, especially in the light of the preceding facts concerning the violation of native and human rights.

2. We call on the Executive of B.C. Conference of the United Church to publically apologize to Earl Maquinna George and his family for its withdrawl of support for his trainig in ministry and immediately provide the funding and other support required for Chief George to complete his ministerial training on his request.

3. We call on the provincial government to conduct a thorough and impartial investigation into the conduct of the Minister of Aboriginal Affairs, the Rev. John Cashore in the above matter and that, until such time as his role has been clarified and cleared of any conflict of interest, he be relieved of his portfolio.

4. We call on the Chief Executive Officer and Directors of MacMillan-Bloedel to demonstrate their good faith for future negotiations with the Ahousahts by returning Lot#363 for the sum of $1.00.

5. We call on the federal government to establish an independent commission of inquiry into a) the collusion of state, church and business in the sale and speculation of native land in Ahousaht, B.C., and b) the particular behaviour of the United Church of Canada in relation to Lot#363 and the alleged abuses and murder at its Ahousaht Residential School., in order to determine whether such behaviour violates the United Church of Canada Act (1925) and the Charities Act (1987), under which the federal government has authorized the United Church to operate.

6. We call upon the membership and clergy of the United Church of Canada to abstain from financially supporting that Church until these matters are publicly rectified and to initiate their own inquiries into the behaviour of those officials described in the above matters.

15 January, 1997
Vancouver, B. C.

The Reverend Kevin D. Annett, B. A., M.A., M. Div.

The Reverend Bruce W. M. Gunn, B.A., B.D., M.A.A.B.S., M. Div.

THE VANCOUVER SUN

Vancouver Sun
Tuesday, June 22, 1999
Editorial
A12
Vaughn Palmer
GLEN CLARK; GORDON CAMPBELL@CORP=MACMILLAN BLOEDEL; WEYERHAEUSER CO.
VICTORIA

Suddenly, it's the NDP defending globalization: American takeover of B.C. icon MacMillan Bloedel is greeted with endoresement of 'world players' in the forest industry.

Vaughn Palmer
Vancouver Sun

VICTORIA - Premier Glen Clark and Opposition leader Gordon Campbell got the word Sunday night, hours before the rest of the province, that B.C.'s largest corporation was being taken over by an American firm.

In confidential briefings arranged by the partners to the takeover, Mr. Campbell learned at 8 p.m. and Mr. Clark two hours later of the impending disappearance of MacMillan Bloedel, a name that looms larger than any other in the province's largest industry.

The new lead dog? Weyerhaeuser, one of the largest U.S. forest companies, headquartered in the Seattle suburb of Federal Way. An odd name that, but I guess British Columbians will have to get used to it. For if the three-and-a-half-billion-dollar takeover goes ahead, the folks from Federal Way will own MacBlo, lock, stock and tree farm licences.

Considering the significance of the deal, the reaction from both leaders was surprisingly blase. Mr. Campbell said he would like more information before offering a final verdict. He also wondered about the fate of MacBlo's workforce and the communities that depend on its mills. But the strongest criticism he could muster was a reflection that it was "a sad day" for the province.

Even that mild lament for the passing of a sizable player in B.C. history eluded the New Democrats. Forests Minister Dave Zirnhelt was quick to dismiss any expressions of "nostalgia" over the end of MacBlo.

"This is about economics," he told reporters. "This isn't about sentimentality . . . . It's one North American company buying another North American company. They are all world players."

Mr. Zirnhelt, who emphasized that he was speaking for the premier as well as for himself, said the government would also like to know more before deciding to approve the takeover. But his initial remarks suggested the Clark government will give the nod -- and cite Weyerhaeuser's willingness to shell out billions as evidence that investors are regaining confidence in the B.C. forest industry.

"It's a good sign that things are turning around for investment in forest products in B.C.," Mr. Zirnhelt said. "If you want to attract capital to B.C., you have to allow your people to be world players . . . . To be world players they have to be effective and they have to be able to command the investments they need to keep up to date."

I'm thinking that must be the strongest defence of globalization ever uttered by a New Democratic Party cabinet minister. And Mr. Zirnhelt had best continue polishing the speech, because, if the rumour mill is correct, the Clark government will be confronted with foreign take-overs of one or two other B.C. forest companies. The Swedes, most notably, are said to be scouting around for a purchase.

The government won't risk driving away those investors, not given the fragile state of the economy in general and the forest industry in particular. But there's a certain irony in the prospect.

Glen Clark cut his teeth in the legislature denouncing the Socreds for allowing the Americans to buy up the relatively small West Kootenay Power and Light. Now he's being forced to rationalize the U.S. acquisition of the largest industrial enterprise in the province.

It should also be noted how Mr. Clark and the NDP had a lot to do with making MacBlo and other forest companies ripe for takeover. The industry's current troubles are rooted in their decisions to raise taxes, increase production costs, slow the flow of lumber and reduce the value of corporate assets.

Not long ago the premier's chief policy adviser, Tom Gunton, was pointing to those changes as evidence that the New Democrats had taken charge of the industry and pointed it in the right direction. In an academic paper published two years ago, Mr. Gunton boasted that "the state has intervened in a manner to reduce the rate of harvest, increase the cost and lower profits of the forest sector." He noted, apparently with pride, how the changes had knocked $3 billion off the value of corporate assets. Yet he went on to insist (echoing the government political line) that the changes would "protect the long-run viability of the forest industry."

You can see the results of the NDP's handiwork in the fate of the largest company of them all, put through the wringer over the past two years and now delivered, giftwrapped by Mr. Clark and his colleagues, into the hands of the Americans.

vpalmer@direct.ca

Figure 18

The Vancouver Sun, MONDAY, DECEMBER 18, 1995

Claim of murder goes back to '40s

A report that a girl was killed by a residential-school official has sparked an investigation.

KAREN GRAM

RCMP are launching an investigation today into an allegation that a young girl was murdered at a United Church residential school for Indians on Vancouver Island 50 years ago.

Art Anderson, an official with the United Church, said Sunday that police were notified of the allegation as soon as the church learned of it.

Rev. Foun McNamee-Annett, a former United Church minister for the Alberni area, reported the allegation to the current minister Thursday. On Friday, both McNamee-Annett and the church lawyer reported it to the police.

"We are uncertain what this means, but we have to treat it seriously," Anderson said. "As of tomorrow, the police will be beginning an investigation."

The investigation was triggered by a statement from a North Vancouver woman who told McNamee-Annett she was nearby when a six-year-old girl was kicked down some stairs and died.

Harriet Nahanee, 60, is the first witness to come forward to support recent allegations about killings at residential schools on the island.

DEADLY NIGHTMARES: Harriet Nahanee, 60, says she is haunted by a murder she witnessed at a United Church residential school in Port Alberni 50 years ago.

In another case, a boy is said to have bled to death after he was beaten as punishment for breaking a jar at the school in Ahousaht in the 1940s.

Reports of sexual and physical assaults at the Port Alberni area school sparked a province-wide investigation of residential schools by an RCMP task force. It has been gathering evidence for about one year.

Please see RCMP, B3

RCMP: Memory sparks tears

Continued from page 1

In an interview with The Vancouver Sun, Nahanee said she can't remember the girl's name but she knows that she came from Nitinat Lake and her father's name was Blackie.

"I remember her from Nitinat Lake," she said. "Every so often her name comes to me and I can see her face."

Nahanee said the girl died in 1946, when Nahanee was 11 years old. But the memory is still painful enough that she cried throughout the telling.

"I was at the bottom of the stairs in the basement," she said. "I always went to the bottom of the stairs to sit and cry.

"I heard her crying, she was looking for her mother. I heard [the school administrator] yelling at the supervisor for letting the child run around on the stairwell.

"I heard him kick her and she fell down the stairs. I went to look — her eyes were open, she wasn't moving. They didn't even come down the stairs.

"They were arguing at the top of the stairs.

"I never saw her again."

Nahanee said other students later told her the girl had died and her body had been sent back to Nitinat Lake.

Nahanee told the other children what she had heard. She told her mother and many of the elders in her tribe. But nobody believed her, the woman said. She didn't trust the RCMP so she didn't report it to them.

Rev. A.E. Caldwell, a United Church minister, was head of the school for the four years Nahanee lived there. She alleges he regularly sexually assaulted her in the infirmary.

In a written statement which has been forwarded to the RCMP task force, Nahanee says she was taken every week to the infirmary where either Caldwell or the boys' supervisor, a Mr. Peake, would force her to perform oral sex.

Nahanee said she believes often deaths, which at the time the church said were the result of exposure when students tried to run away, were really caused by beatings in the school town.

The woman still has nightmares about the killing and lives with rage and shame resulting from her treatment.

"I would love to be free of the shame — to leave all that behind me and have some pride in myself."

Figure 19

Beaten to death for theft of a prune

Indian elder recalls strapping of 15-year-old boy at Island residential school in 1938 by United Church minister.

MARK HUME
Vancouver Sun

A 15-year-old boy who stole a prune from a jar in the kitchen of a United Church residential school was strapped so relentlessly his kidneys failed him and he later died in bed, says a native Indian elder who was there at the time.

Archie Frank, now 68, was just 11 years old when his school mate, Albert Gray, was caught stealing in the Ahousat Residential School kitchen one night in 1938.

Frank, a retired commercial fisher, says he's never forgotten what happened to Gray, a husky youngster from the remote Vancouver Island community of Nitinat.

"He got strapped to death," said Frank in an interview on Tuesday.

"Just for stealing one prune, [Rev. A.E.] Caldwell strapped him to death.

"Beat the s—— right out of him."

Frank's story, told after a 57-year silence, crystallizes much of what the furore over residential schools is all about.

For the past year the RCMP has been probing a series of alleged abuses at church-run residential schools. So far they have found evidence that 54 people were victims of abuse at the hands of 94 offenders. The investigation is concerned with 14 residential schools operated by the Anglican, United and Roman Catholic churches from the late 1800s to 1984.

The First United Church has come under scrutiny by the RCMP this week because of new allegations that two children were killed while at the residential school in the Port Alberni area in the 1940s and '50s.

Frank said Caldwell left Ahousat after the residential school burned down in 1940 and went on to be principal of the United Church school in Port Alberni.

Please see SCHOOL, A2

SCHOOL: Beaten to death for theft of a prune

Continued from page 1

Frank said Gray was caught with his hand in the prune jar by the night watchman at the Ahousat school.

"The day after he got strapped so badly he couldn't get out of bed. The strap wore through a half inch of his skin.

"His kidneys gave out. He couldn't hold his water anymore," said Frank, who has never told his story to the police.

He said Gray lay in his bed for several weeks after the beating, while he and another boy at the school cared for him, bringing him meals, and changing the urine-soaked sheets on his bed.

"They wouldn't bring him to a doctor. I don't think they wanted to reveal the extent of his injuries," said Frank, who still lives in the tiny village of Ahousat, just outside Tofino on the west coast of Vancouver Island.

Frank said he spent several years attending the First United Church residential school in Ahousat, and for the most part found it to be a good place.

"I had a very good experience in that school.

"That was the only one [bad incident] I experienced," said Frank of the death of his friend.

He said he never thought of reporting the death at the time because he was only 11 years old and because the principal of the school was seen as the ultimate authority.

When he grew older he sometimes remembered Gray, he said, but didn't go to the police because his philosophy was: "Keep out of harm's way — and learn to forgive."

Frank was asked why he thought a boy would be beaten so severely for such a minor offence.

"I don't know how you guys operate. That's not the Indian way," he replied.

Frank also said there seems little point because Caldwell is now dead.

"There's no use having hard feelings for a dead man. If he was alive, I'd still be angry," he said.

Rev. Bruce Gunn, the United Church minister in Ahousat, said Frank's attitude of forgiveness is typical of the older generation of Indian people.

"Their tradition was to get along because they lived in survival cultures. They knew how important it was to forgive," he said.

But Gunn said younger Indian people feel it's important to get to the bottom of what happened, and they are pressing for inquiries into crimes that may have happened more than 50 years ago.

Gunn said he has been talking to elders in Ahousat, trying to confirm some of the stories that have been going around.

He hadn't talked to Frank, but said he would.

Attention was drawn to the United Church residential school system on Vancouver Island earlier this month when Jack McDonald, a candidate for the New Democratic Party leadership, called for a public inquiry into alleged deaths at schools in the Port Alberni area.

McDonald said he'd heard of at least two deaths, one of which was in Ahousat.

Sgt. Paul Willms, who is heading the RCMP investigation into abuse at B.C. residential schools, said he hadn't heard any allegations about deaths in the Port Alberni area until McDonald brought them up.

The police in Port Alberni this week began questioning witnesses and promised a thorough investigation.

Meanwhile, Kevin McNamee-Annett, a former United Church minister, issued a statement Monday saying he's going on a fast to protest against the church's handling of the issue.

Vancouver Sun, December 20, 1995

Figure 20

An eyewitness account of one of these killings, of student Albert Gray by United Church Principal Alfred Caldwell at the Ahousaht Indian school (1995)

The Vancouver Sun

THURSDAY, FEBRUARY 1, 1996

15 Indian men seek millions

Rapes, beatings 30 years ago at Island residential school are the basis of a lawsuit against Ottawa, United Church.

MARK HUME
Vancouver Sun

A series of rapes and beatings that shocked a B.C. Supreme Court judge are the basis for a massive lawsuit by 15 men against the federal government, the United Church of Canada and four administrators.

The case, filed in Vancouver on Tuesday, claims unspecified damages for a series of brutal physical and sexual assaults that took place at the Port Alberni Indian Residential School during the 1960s.

Vancouver lawyer Peter Grant said that he could not put a specific dollar figure to the claim, but believes it will become the biggest suit of its kind ever filed in Canada.

"For any one of the victims the claim would be for a large amount of money. For all of them it would be massive," he said.

"We have 15 individuals here whose lives have been destroyed."

By way of comparison, Grant said that his clients would be seeking "a lot more" than the $50 million former prime minister Brian Mulroney is seeking in a libel suit against the federal government.

"I wonder what he would have sued for if he'd lost 30 years of his life," said Grant.

"When you look at the pleadings in this case, the destruction to each of these people is immense. One of the victims was beaten so much he became deaf. Most never finished school because of what happened to them. They've suffered the problems of divorce, alcohol abuse, drug addiction. One described today how he can't control his bowels whenever he's under stress, because of what happened to him."

The suit follows the conviction last March of Arthur Henry Plint, who was given 11 years in jail for a series of sexual assaults that took place 30 years ago at the Alberni residential school.

Plint, who was supervisor of the boys' dorms at the school, repeatedly abused the children in his care.

The courts heard that when some of the children complained to other school officials, they were ostracized or beaten.

When B.C. Supreme Court Justice Douglas Hogarth heard the case against Plint, he said he was shocked.

"I must say that I have now been in this business since 1950 as a lawyer and primarily in criminal law, and since on the bench, and I have never se...

Please see LAWSUIT.

Figure 21

Report of the first class action lawsuit brought by residential school students against the United Church and government of Canada (1996)

208

271453

R E G U L A T I O N. No. 4.

Any person shall be guilty of an offence and shall be liable to a fine not exceeding ten dollars and costs who wilfully manufactures or posts up any obscene pictures or obscene carvings upon any building bridge, fence, tree box or other thing in any place open to the public or to be seen by the public in the Indian village of Port Simpson.

(sgnd) Alfred Dudoward
Chief Councillor.

(sgnd) Chas Todd
Indian Agent.

Figure 22

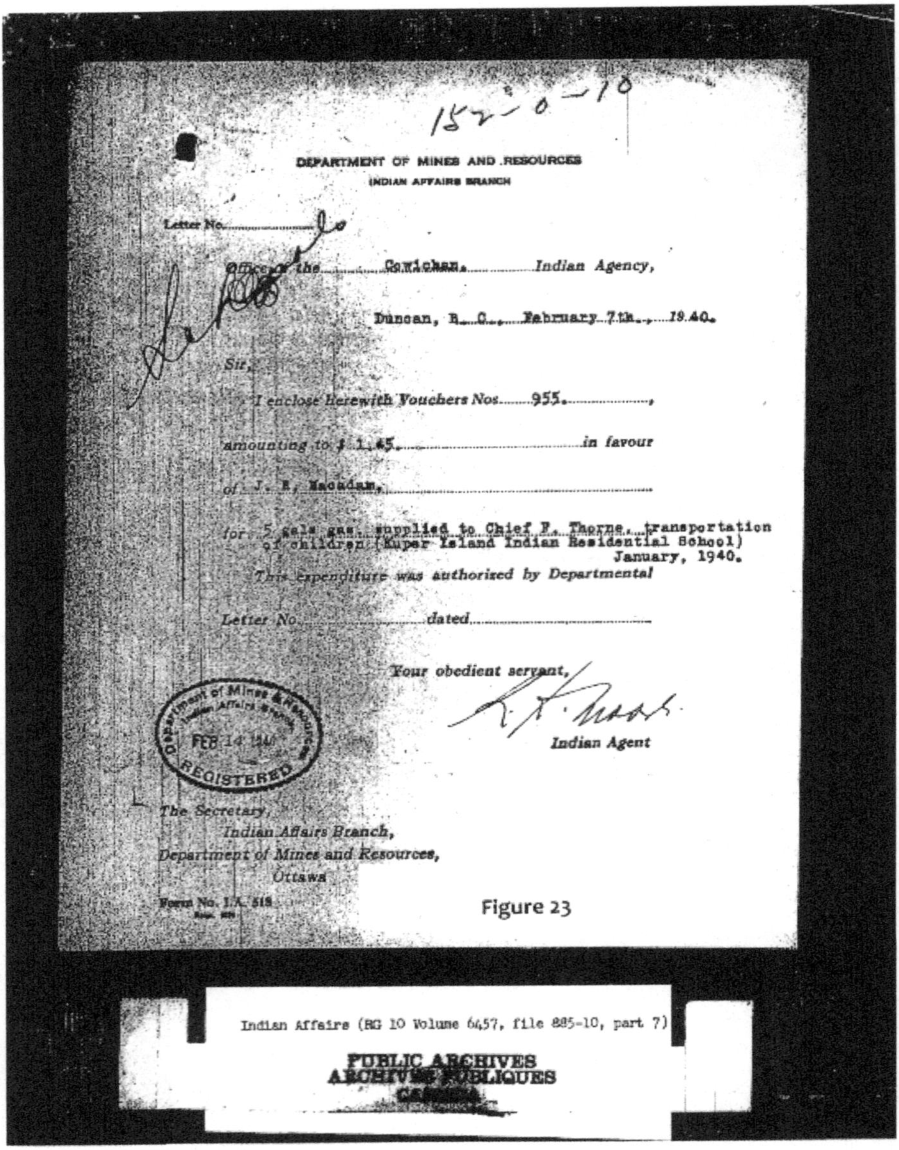

152-0-10

DEPARTMENT OF MINES AND RESOURCES

INDIAN AFFAIRS BRANCH

Letter No.........

Office of the Cowichan. Indian Agency,

Duncan, B. C., February 7th., 19.40.

Sir,

I enclose herewith Vouchers Nos 955.,

amounting to $ 1.45. in favour

of J. R. Macadam,

for 5 gals gas, supplied to Chief F. Thorne, transportation of children (Kuper Island Indian Residential School) January, 1940.

This expenditure was authorized by Departmental

Letter No.......... dated..........

Your obedient servant,

Indian Agent

Department of Mines & Resources, Indian Affairs Branch, FEB 14 1940, REGISTERED

The Secretary,
Indian Affairs Branch,
Department of Mines and Resources,
Ottawa

Form No. I.A. 518

Indian Affairs (RG 10 Volume 6457, file 885-10, part 7)

PUBLIC ARCHIVES
ARCHIVES PUBLIQUES
CANADA

Figure 23

Appendix One: A Chronology of the Crime

7000 BCE: The ancestors of the Ahousaht people migrate southward from Asia along the west coast of North America in the wake of a post-glaciation warming.

3000 BCE: The Ahousahts are established as the predominant cultural group on the western central region of "Vancouver Island", covering a settlement area of hundreds of miles. Their population will reach a probable maximum of more than 25,000 people prior to the European contact that will shrink their numbers to a few hundred. The Ahousahts are a fishing and a whaling tribal society with inherited stratified lineages and a settled subsistence economy.

1450 - 1600 CE: Contact is made between the Ahousahts and Chinese, Japanese and possibly English sailing fleets, according to the "whites before the whites" oral history accounts of Ahousaht elders.

1778 CE: The first prolonged European contact with the Ahousahts is made by British Captain James Cook in Nootka

Sound. Over four weeks, the British trade and make contact with the Ahousaht chieftains.

1788: The first fur trade among the Ahousahts is launched by British merchant seaman Captain James Strange. Several trade agreements are made at Yuquot by the British with Ahousaht Chiefs Maquinna and Wickanninish.

1789: Spanish vessels arrive at Yuquot and the Spaniards build a fur trading fort. Armed conflict breaks out between the British and the Spaniards. The Ahousaht chiefs are pressured by both nations to take sides. In response the Ahousahts, led by Chief Maquinna, shun the Europeans and impede their fur trade.

1791-92: The Spanish pit Ahousaht chief Wickanninish against Maquinna by giving the former a share in their fur trade. Civil war begins among the Ahousahts as the two factions battle for control of the trade. The Spanish and British jointly sign the Nootka Convention in an attempt to peacefully divide up the fur trade and maintain amicable relations with the Ahousahts and other west coast tribes essential for the fur trade. But Maquinna seeks to limit European expansion in his territory, opposed by Wickanninish and other chiefs.

1794-96: Internicine warfare between coastal Indians and Europeans continues, including the Royal Navy shelling of Ahousaht villages. The local fur trade goes into decline as most of the otters are killed and the trade moves north. The Spanish fort at Yuquot is abandoned and the Spaniards depart from the region. But British trading posts at Yuquot expand and some settlement begins on traditional Ahousaht lands, as the British begin to cultivate the fishing and whaling industries.

1803: In retaliation for the continued European incursions Maquinna leads a war party in Nootka Sound that captures and destroys the American whaling ship *Boston*, killing all of its crew save two sailors who become Maquinna's slaves.

1800-1850: British settlements spread all over Ahousaht territory. Coastal tribes engage in continual warfare with one another over control of the brokering of whales and fish to the British. In 1849 the British crown colony of Victoria is established on Vancouver Island after the Americans cede the region to England.

1850-1870: As the whaling industry goes into decline by 1865, the first smallpox epidemics begin among the Ahousahts. They are deliberately spread by Anglican missionaries and agents of the Puget Sound Agricultural Company (PSAC).

The Ahousaht population declines quickly by over 90% in a few years, similar to other induced epidemics among northern and interior British Columbia Indian tribes. Ahousaht chief Matlahaw attempts to kill Catholic missionary August Brabant for introducing smallpox-infected blankets among members of his rebellious Hesquait band.

1886-1895: With the linking of the west coast with the rest of Canada by the Canadian Pacific Railway, European missionaries and settlers pour into the Ahousaht region. In 1891 Prebyterian missionary and land speculator Melvin Swartout arrives in the Ahouaht heartland. Catholic Bishop Auguste Brabant attempts to incite the Ahousahts against the Presbyterians, adding to the existing factionalism among the remnant Ahousaht tribe which now numbers barely a few hundred people.

1903-4: Melvin Swartout surveys and purchases Ahousaht lands for the Presbyterian church. In July 1904 he is found dead, possibly murdered, but no investigation is made either by his Presbyterian Church or the government. Swartout's fellow missionary John Ross arrives in Ahousaht the same year, armed with the powers of a policeman and a provincial magistrate. Ross opens the first residential school for Ahousaht children and establishes a native police force to discipline and arrest errant Ahousahts. Over half of the Ahousahts are still not Christianized, the highest percentage of remaining non- Christian "pagans" anywhere in British Columbia.

1907: Government health inspector Dr. Peter Bryce investigates Indian schools across western Canada, including in the Ahousht region, and discovers that an average 30% to 60% of the students are dying while incarcerated in them. In a report made public in November, Bryce states,
"I believe the conditions are being deliberately created to

spread infectious disease". Bryce's findings are suppressed by the government and he is forced out of the civil service.

1910: As Principal of the Ahousaht residential school, John Ross conducts a one-man war against Chief Maquinna and Chief Billy August, who resist Christian conversion and refuse to send their children into the residential school. These chiefs and others are fined and arrested by Ross for conducting traditional potlatching ceremonies. The same year, the federal government signs a formal contract with the Catholic, Anglican and Presbyterian-Methodist churches to jointly fund and operate Indian residential schools across Canada.

1914: Ahousaht elders unsuccessfuly petition the federal government to have Ross removed as school Principal.

1916: Ross resigns as school Principal after being implicated in the violent death of Chief Billy August's daughter Carrie George. Indian Agent Cox exonerates Ross of any wrong doing. Ross assumes the Principalship of the nearby Ucluelet Indian day school.

Summer-Fall 1917: Ahousaht residential school is burned to the ground. John Ross returns to build a new school. Ross then attempts to sell the new building and the land it occupies, known as Lot 363, to the federal government on behalf of the Presbyterian Church. The latter ask for $2000, or $200 an acre, for a ten acre parcel of the land, despite the land's assessment at $15 an acre. The government refuses this exorbitant price, and Ross leaves Ahousaht for good, returning to Ucluelet.

July 1, 1920: Despite the consistently enormous death rates in the Indian residential schools, the federal government enacts an Order in Council making it mandatory for all native children seven years and older to be placed in the schools, on pain of parental fine and imprisonment. The death rate in these schools soars, including after all regular medical inspection is curtailed by the government. Over the next decade, the operating churches will be made the legal guardians of residential school students, sexual sterilization laws against Indians are promulgated, and Indians are denied the right to hire lawyers and appear in Canadian courts of law.

1925: The United Church of Canada is formed by an Act of Parliament, merging the Presbyterian and Methodist churches. The new United Church inherits all of the property and Indian residential schools of these churches, including the Ahousaht facility and the Lot 363 on which is stands. The United Church's stated mandate includes "Canadianizing and Christianizing the foreigner and the pagan".

1953: The grandson of missionary John Ross, a local businessman named Hamilton Ross who is a United Church member, is sold all of Lot 363 in Ahousaht by the United Church for a mere $2000, or $10 an acre: one twentieth the price asked by the church for the same land in 1917.

1956: Hamilton Ross sells Lot 363 to the United Church's corporate partner and financial benefactor, MacMillan-Bloedel Ltd., the largest logging company in B.C., for $6000: triple the price he bought it for from the church.

July 1992: Rev. Kevin Annett begins his ministry as pastor of St. Andrew's United Church in Port Alberni, and begins work among many local Indians, including Ahousahts and residential school survivors.

November 1992: Ahousaht Chief Earl Maquinna George, the descendent of Chief Billy August and the hereditary elder responsible for protecting Ahousaht lands, writes to the government of B.C. Earl demands the return of Lot 363 to his people as part of the current land claims negotiations. The government then places a moratorium on further logging in Ahousaht until Earl's claim is addressed.

February-June 1993: A series of secret meetings between Ahousaht band council chiefs and officials of MacMillan-Bloedel, the United Church and the government of B.C. secures the support of the Ahousahts for the sale to Mac-Blo of Lot 363 and other Ahousaht land in return for the creation of a Joint Ventures company, Lissak Ltd., to be 51% owned by some of the Ahousaht chiefs. Earl George is not informed of these meetings. In the same period, the United Church suspends its previous funding and support for Earl George's approved ministerial training.

December 10, 1993: The government's Provincial Interim Measures Agreement (PIMA) governing aboriginal land claims is signed in Victoria, funding local native bands in return for their approval of "internal free trade agreements" with foreign corporations. Earl George is a signatory but he continues to oppose the sale of Lot 363.

January 10, 1994: Earl George is notified by two United Church officials, Cameron Reid and Colin Forbes, that he is no longer a candidate for United Church ministry, without giving a reason. Earl retires into seclusion.

October 17, 1994: Rev. Kevin Annett writes a letter to the Comox-Nanaimo Presbytery of the United Church. He opposes the sale of Lot 363 and calls for its unconditional return without cost to the Ahousaht people. Kevin cites United Church policy that requires such a course of action. He never receives a reply.

October 23, 1994: Kevin's letter is discussed on the United Church's General Council in Toronto. The Council appoints the same two United Church officials who sidelined Earl George from his ministry, Cameron Reid and Colin Forbes, along with B.C. Conference officials Bill Howie and Art Anderson, to begin secret proceedings to have Kevin Annett removed from his Port Alberni pulpit and expelled from church ministry.

January 23, 1995: United Church personnel officer Art Anderson and Cameron Reid hand Kevin Annett a letter of dismissal that immediately removes him from his position without cause. The letter requires that he agree to "psychiatric evaluation" and unpaid "pastoral retraining", or face permanent "delisting" (expulsion) as a United Church minister. Kevin receives no notice or review of his ministry prior to his firing, as required under United Church policy.

June 1995: Lot 363 is fully acquired by MacMillan-Bloedel. Kevin Annett and his family are evicted from the church manse and move from Port Alberni. Kevin's wife Anne McNamee is encouraged and funded to divorce him and win custody of his children in a divorce trial paid for by the United Church of Canada. Kevin is denied the right to apply for employment elsewhere in the United Church and faces a years-long blacklisting and smear campaign by the church and the RCMP.

September 1996-March 1997: Kevin Annett is "delisted" in a public show trial at the cost to the church of $300,000. He is denied due process and natural justice during the trial, which is chaired by the same man who arranged Kevin's dismissal in 1995, church lawyer Jon Jessiman. His delisting is final and cannot be appealed.

November 1999: Weyerhauser Ltd. acquires MacMillan-Bloedel in the largest corporate takeover in British Columbia history, totalling over $2 billion.

Spring 2000: The Joint Venture company, Lissak Ltd., is fully acquired by chiefs on the Ahousaht band council and proceeds to log off the last of the old growth red cedar forests in the Clayoquot Sound.

July 2003: Earl Maquinna George dies after lingering from the effects of a stroke.

Appendix Two: An Important Note on Sources

My main source for this book, of course, is my own experience living and working among the Ahousahts, first as a clergyman of the United Church that destroyed them and then, after my violent expulsion from it, as a defender of its victims and a chronicler of its west coast genocide.

Agreeing with Emerson that "All history is biography, for the whole of history is found in one man", I have tried to illuminate the still-denied and obfuscated Group Crime of my people through the lives of its victims and perpetrators: but especially among those who crossed my path as it wound its own troubled way through the land of the Ahousahts.

One of the few pleasures enjoyed by former insiders like me who turn whistle blower is our capacity to provoke an irrational hysteria among our persecutors simply by opening our mouths and telling what happened. This has proven especially true when it comes to yours truly and the United Church of Canada and its corporate partners in crime.

Any publication that has ever dared to print my tale and the facts of the Lot 363 deal has faced immediate threats and censure by that church and its battery of lawyers, from *Canadian Dimension* magazine to the innocuous tabloid newspaper the *Vancouver Courier* to the famed London based *New Internationalist* magazine. My former clerical colleagues just don't want that story told, and for very good reason: because it follows the money behind their crime. Saul Alinsky, the inveterate community organizer, may have been referring to the United Church of Canada when he remarked, "Evil has an address, and its inhabitants don't want you knocking on their door."

Some of the church's palaver over our story comes from the fact that it upsets the official narrative because it doesn't rely on the usual controlled sources. For generations, a hired stable of Canadian academics have studiously camouflaged the hard reality of genocide in their own back yard by fudging the body count, muting the witnesses and upholding the church's official myth of well-intentioned purpose towards Indians.

One poignant example stands out for me. I recall with a sad amusement the blank look on the face of my academic advisor Dr. Jean Barman when, during my brief tenure as a doctoral student at the University of B.C. after my expulsion from the United Church, I showed her the records of Dr. Peter Bryce. The records indicated that over half the children in the residential schools were being deliberately killed after their routine infection with disease. "But that's not possible" is all she said. So much for academia.

Such learned disbelief toward our own Group Crime runs solidly through the different "scholarly" sources concerning the Ahousahts, our theft of their land and annihilation of their nation and their children. I have therefore only minimally relied on those sources, turning instead not only to the Ahousahts and their own oral and written histories but to recent writers who make an attempt to look more at the genocidal practices on the west coast.

Two of these writers are Chris Arnett (no relation, I think) and Tom Swanky. Chris Arnett's interesting book **The Terror of the Coast: Land Alienation and Colonial War on Vancouver**

Island and the Gulf Islands, 1849-1863 (2010) suffers from the usual mainstream academic limitation of focusing on only one scale of the dragon (or shall I say, Octopus). But within this restriction he shows in detail some of the British pulverising of rebellious Cowichan tribes on Vancouver Island.

Tom Swanky's less scholarly but intricate detailing of the inoculating to death of vast swaths of British Columbia Indians by roving, smallpox-spreading Anglican missionaries - **The True Story of Canada's War of Extermination on the Pacific** (2013) - leaves no doubt concerning the historic criminality of Christian churches on this land.

Despite the paucity of genuine studies of the Canadian west coast genocide, I have included below a brief anthology of useful articles and books on the Ahousahts and the history in their territory from contact to the present day.

And finally, of course, I have relied on the most thorough independent account of the Canadian Holocaust in general, which is my own twenty years of research contained in my work **Murder by Decree: The Crime of Genocide in Canada**.

(2016) Most of the documents found in the present book come from that tome, and from the hundreds of long hours I spent poring through the microfilmed archives of the Department of Indian Affairs in the UBC Koerner Library. The latter bibliotheca was named, ironically, after Walter Koerner, a German-born industrial robber baron who made his fortune by annihilating much of the old growth forest on Vancouver Island, including on the Ahousahts' land.

Murder most foul does come out, it seems, thanks especially to the ones who caused it.

A Brief Anthology of works on the Ahousahts and related matters

Annett, Kevin D., **Murder by Decree: The Crime of Genocide in Canada - A Counter Report to the 'Truth and Reconicliation Commission'** (Amazon Books, 2016) and **Unrelenting: Between Sodom and Zion** (ibid)

Arnett, Chris, **The Terror of the Coast: Land Alienation and Colonial War on Vancouver Island and the Gulf Islands, 1849-1863** (Talon Books, 2010)

Bridge, Kathryn and Kevin Neary, **Voices of the Elders: Huu-ay-aht Histories and Legends** (Nuu-Chah-Nulth Tribal Council, Port Alberni, 2013)

Kennedy, Mervyn Ewart, **The History of Presbyterianism in British Columbia, 1861-1935** (M.A. Thesis, UBC Department of History, 1938) (View online pdf at this UBC archive site: *file:///C:/Users/User/Downloads/UBC_1938_A8%20K3%20H5.pdf*)

Marshall, Yvonne May, **A Political History of the Nuu-Chah-Nulth People: A case Study of the Mowachaht and Muchalahy Tribes** (M.A. Thesis, Simon Fraser University, 1987)

Swanky, Tom, **The True Story of Canada's War of Extermination on the Pacific** (Dragon Heart Books, 2013)

Oral History sources on the Ahousahts:

Chief Earl Maquinna George, Chief Nelson Keitlah, Elder Alfred Keitlah, Bruce W. Gunn, Sadie Ambrose, Krista Lynn, Karl Angus, Jack McDonald, Particia Louie and Albert Sam

About the Author

Kevin Annett is an award-winning author, film maker and global human rights campaigner. A former ordained minister of the United Church of Canada, Kevin was fired without cause from his church and expelled from his profession without due process between 1995 and 1997 because of his challenging of the land profiteering and crimes of genocide by his church against west coast indigenous people. Since 1998 he has led the campaign to expose and prosecute crimes against children by Church and State, first in Canada and then abroad. Kevin is a founding Director of the International Tribunal of Crimes of Church and State (ITCCS), which helped prosecute and depose Pope Benedict in 2013 for Crimes against Humanity. Kevin is the author of more than a dozen books and is a highly acclaimed public speaker, spiritual advisor and community organizer. He has been nominated twice for the Nobel Peace Prize by American scholars.

Kevin's websites include www.KevinAnnett.com , www.murderbydecree.com and www.itccs.org . He can be contacted at thecommonland@gmail.com or through 386-323-5774 (USA).

Made in United States
North Haven, CT
07 June 2023